CERTIFIED
ANGUS
BEEF®

The Art of Cooking with Certified Angus Beef

A Collection of Recipes by Distinguished Chefs

Certified Angus Beef Committee Message

Certified Angus Beef, a non-profit program of the American Angus Association, was implemented to facilitate the marketing of high quality beef from Angus-type cattle. The program includes the evaluation of beef carcasses by the United States Department of Agriculture's Grading Service, based upon stringent beef quality specifications. The primary concern of the Certified Angus Beef Program is to assure beef buyers of consistent, high quality whenever beef labeled with the federally registered Certified Angus Beef trademark is purchased. "The Art of Cooking with Certified Angus Beef" has been published to recognize the selected chefs' extraordinary culinary talents and share them with all who appreciate high quality beef and beautiful presentations.

Dedication

"The Art of Cooking with Certified Angus Beef" is proudly dedicated to three individuals whose dedication and commitment to the Certified Angus Beef Program's success has been unsurpassed.

Professor Leonard Berkowitz: Florida International University, Miami, Florida; consultant for Certified Angus Beef; responsible for the program's introduction to the food service industry.

Mr.Fred Johnson: Summitcrest Farms, Summitville, Ohio; registered Angus cattle breeder; member and past chairman of the original Certified Angus Beef Board of Directors.

Dr. B.D. VanStavern: Professor Emeritus, Animal Science, The Ohio State University, Columbus, Ohio; developed Certified Angus Beef specifications; advisor to the Certified Angus Beef Board of Directors.

Published by CULINAIRE, INC. for CERTIFIED ANGUS BEEF, P.O. Box 819, West Salem, Ohio 44287

Project Coordinator: **Bill Wylie**
Director, Food Service Division
Certified Angus Beef

Photographer: **Franz Mitterer**
Writers: **Anne Byrn**
James L. Miller, CEC
Illustrator: **Jennifer Haberstock**
Book Design: **Robert Hosley**

Library of Congress Catalog Card Number: 89-61562

ISBN 0-9623729-0-0

Printed in Hong Kong

Message from the Executive Director

Louis M. "Mick" Colvin
Executive Director, Certified Angus Beef

Mick Colvin (right) enjoys a glass of champagne at Le Bec Fin with Chef/Owner Georges Perrier.

The American Angus Association is especially proud to introduce this beautiful cookbook, "The Art of Cooking with Certified Angus Beef." We are pleased to be able to offer this book as a return contribution to the food service industry. After all, it was as a result of the request from discriminating chefs for a higher quality, more consistent beef product that the Certified Angus Beef Program was born.

For over a decade now I have been personally involved in the Certified Angus Beef Program and have watched it develop from infancy into the great success it is today. Certified Angus Beef is delighted to be an integral part of the success of thousands of restaurants worldwide, and we're proud to put our trademark on a product that enhances the palatability of so many dishes. Thanks to outstanding chefs and their restaurants, as well as our family of packers, fabricators, food service distributors and retailers, for making the Certified Angus Beef Program the largest specification-branded beef program in the world.

We firmly believe that a product must have true added value to be successful. Certified Angus Beef has such value - thanks to strict specifications. We set standards to insure superior palatability, and we have adhered to them since the program's inception. Beef may be touted as "coming back," but the reason people eat beef has not changed - people enjoy juicy, tender, flavorful beef! Certified Angus Beef specifications are designed to identify such a product. If representatives of other so-called "programs" say their beef is "just as good as Certified Angus Beef," simply compare the specifications. You will find it's like comparing a reproduction to a rare oil painting.

And when prepared by gifted artists like those chefs included in this cookbook, Certified Angus Beef rises to new heights. Chefs are like artists, and when Certified Angus Beef is their canvas, they are able to create true masterpieces. "The Art of Cooking with Certified Angus Beef" is an apt title for a collection of recipes so carefully constructed and beautifully photographed. They are feasts for the eye as well as the palate.

To our featured chefs and many others, thank you for the challenge and the inspiration!

Cookbook Contributors

Jean Banchet
Raymond Bertschy
Paul Bocuse
Gerhard Brill
Charles Carroll
Thomas Catherall
Roland Czekelius
Ralph DiOrio
Tell Erhardt
John Farnsworth
Lawrence Forgione
Denise Fugo
Michael Garbin
William Hahne
Henry Haller
Hartmut Handke
Naoe Hirota
Raimund Hofmeister
William Jung
Peter Loren
Arthur Mangie
Joe Mannke
John McCormick
Gerald Messerli
Walter Meyer
James Miller
Mark Miller
C.T. Nice
Georges Perrier
Christian Rassinoux
Patrizio Sacchetto
Joseph Saget
August Schreiner
Thomas Semke
André Soltner
David Spadafore
Nicola Torres
Lucien Vendome
Lawrence Vito
Takashi Wada
Babe's Steakhouse
John Q's Public Bar & Grille
Plaza III Restaurant
Scotch 'n Sirloin
Taste of Texas
Gibbet Hill Farm
Irvington Farms
Octoraro Farm

Table of Contents

In preparing this book, Certified Angus Beef asked chefs to not only feature recipes using the traditional middle meat (rib & loin) cuts but to also use end meat (chuck & round) items. Thus, the cookbook illustrates the versatility of Certified Angus Beef and demonstrates a wide application of those sometimes under-utilized items.

The American Institute of Wine & Food

K. Dun Gifford
Chairman

George E. Munger
Vice Chairman

Dorothy Cann
Secretary

Michael McCarty
Treasurer

Julia Child
Robert Mondavi
Honorary Chairmen

Richard H. Graff
William W. Young
Chairmen Emeritus

1550 Bryant Street, San Francisco, California 94103
Telephone: (415) 255-3000
FAX: (415) 255-2874

The American Institute of Wine and Food is delighted to participate with Certified Angus Beef and the leading chefs from around the country who worked together to present this fine and exciting book, "The Art of Cooking with Certified Angus Beef." Since many of these chefs are members of the AIWF and since the book's author, Anne Byrn, has been a key leader in the AIWF for some years, it is fitting that the AIWF join with the Certified Angus Beef Program to carry forward the book's educational message.

The chefs who offer us their knowledge and experience in these pages have earned their impeccable reputations by insisting on the highest quality products for their kitchens, and then cooking these products with imagination and skill before sending them out to their dining rooms. A key ingredient of the success of these chefs is their ability to identify reliable and credible sources of high quality supplies for their kitchens.

A certification program is an invaluable tool in this search, and the certification program instituted in 1978 by the American Angus Association for Certified Angus Beef has made a major mark in the beef industry and in the food service industry in only a few short years. The AIWF, in its educational programs directed at quality, has always been supportive of certification, and for this reason the continuing work of the American Angus Association, working with the U.S. Department of Agriculture, holds powerful and important lessons for all of us.

K. Dun Gifford
Chairman of the Board

United States
Department of
Agriculture

Agricultural
Marketing
Service

P.O. Box 96456
Washington, DC
20090-6456

March 8, 1989

Certified Angus Beef
Post Office Box 819
West Salem, Ohio 44287

Dear Certified Angus Beef staff:

I want to congratulate the American Angus Association and specifically the Certified Angus Beef program for its most recent endeavor--the publishing of a Certified Angus Beef cookbook.

We at the United States Department of Agriculture (USDA) are very proud of our involvement with the Certified Angus Beef program. Our relationship with Certified Angus Beef was initiated in the late 1970's and continues today, as strong as ever. We believe that Certified Angus Beef's use of USDA's certification service has been an exceptional mechanism to identify an "elite" segment of the beef supply which is consistently tender, juicy, and flavorful. We know from our experience in writing meat grade standards and meat purchase specifications, that a standard or specification which CONSISTENTLY identifies a uniform product can make a significant contribution toward the successful marketing of that product. The "G1" specification utilized in the Certified Angus Beef program is a prime example of such a specification. Through the success of Certified Angus Beef, "G1" has proved its ability to consistently identify beef with delightful eating characteristics.

Let me again congratulate Certified Angus Beef on its effort to print a cookbook and reiterate USDA's belief that programs such as Certified Angus Beef play an important role in providing consistently high quality beef to America's consuming public.

Sincerely,
Michael L. May

Michael L. May
Chief
Livestock and Meat Standardization Branch

The Agricultural Marketing Service
is an agency of the
United States Department of Agriculture

A Tradition of Excellence

THE CERTIFIED ANGUS BEEF STORY

"The Angus Breed is Launched in America." This oil painting by artist Frank Murphy commemorated in 1973 the 100th anniversary of Angus cattle in the United States. London silk merchant George Grant imported the first Aberdeen-Angus cattle to improve the native Longhorns.

In virtually all areas of business, a new, improved model comes along and surpasses the competition. In the beef industry, that leader is Certified Angus Beef - beef so superior that it has passed scrupulous evaluations for quality and is regarded as the best money can buy.

It was little more than a decade ago that Certified Angus Beef, from cattle descending from the esteemed Scottish Angus herds, was first introduced to the American home dinner table ... and four years later to the growing restaurant sector.

From the very beginning, Angus cattle were developed as the "butcher's breed," yielding beef a breed apart from Choice because inherent quality traits in Angus cattle produce highly palatable beef. For one, marbling occurs at a young age without the development of too much external, waste fat. It was these traits, coupled with product specifications certified by the United States Department of Agriculture's (USDA) grading service, that the American Angus Association decided to utilize when designing a high quality brand of beef targeted at quite a different market segment than typical, commodity beef.

Certified Angus Beef was launched in 1978 by the American Angus Association to enable consumers to purchase a consistent, high quality, specification-branded beef product at licensed restaurants and food stores. More specifically, Certified Angus Beef is a federally registered trademark owned by the American Angus Association, the largest beef breed registry association in the world, a nonprofit organization of some 25,000 ranchers, breeders and feeders of registered Angus cattle.

The Certified Angus Beef Program was born on October 19, 1978 in a small retail store in Columbus, Ohio, where the product was first test marketed. And it has grown into a program that, although it doesn't own the cattle or the beef product, works to license establishments which process, distribute and merchandise product under the Certified Angus Beef label.

When compared to Prime beef, Certified Angus Beef proves to be more consistent in quality, more readily available in most markets and priced very attractively. Yet, production and sales growth of Certified Angus Beef may better explain the story. Thousands of restaurants

throughout the United States and numerous foreign countries serve Certified Angus Beef. And the highly selective program for securing and branding this beef is the largest of its kind in the world.

An event took place in 1976 that was the catalyst for the Certified Angus Beef Program. The USDA was petitioned by the National Cattleman's Association to lower its beef quality grading standards. That meant that older cattle and cattle with less marbling might be sold as Choice. At the same time, the volume of Prime beef began to decline. Certified Angus Beef set forth to fill the void created by the lowering of the beef quality grading standards and to answer the food service industry's demand for a consistent, high quality beef product.

The Certified Angus Beef Program was established to identify cattle superior to those whose carcasses might be graded simply USDA Choice. Today about half of the carcasses produced by the U.S. fed cattle supply are federally graded, and approximately 90 percent of those grade Choice. But of that number, more than 70 percent fall into the lowest acceptable marbling range for USDA Choice. In contrast, Certified Angus Beef accepts only the highest two marbling levels (the upper 30 percent) of the USDA Choice grade, from carcasses of Angus-type cattle.

The Angus cattle breed originated in Scotland. Here, the successors of that early breed graze at Gibbet Hill Farm in Groton, Massachusetts in early spring.

5

The Certified Angus Beef Story

While most cattle are finished in the high plains area today, Angus seedstock producers are 25,000 members strong in all 50 states. One such producer is Irvington Farms in West Point, Georgia.

Angus cattle have an interesting history, dating back to early Scotland and England, where hearty meat-eaters demanded top quality steaks and roasts. The hornless, black-hided cattle were most likely brought to England when the Celtic people migrated from southwest Europe.

Two counties in Scotland - Aberdeenshire and Angusshire - developed hornless strains of cattle. From these strains the Aberdeen-Angus breed resulted, and for simplicity the name was shortened to Angus. The breed withstood competition from crossbreeds. Instead, through slow, methodical, selective breeding by men such as Hugh Watson of Keillor, Scotland, considered a pioneer and the Angus breed "improver," Angus cattle developed many of the traits that make them so important today.

The autumn foliage presents the perfect backdrop for these Angus cows and their weanling-size calves at Octoraro Farm, Nottingham, Pennsylvania.

Angus cattle made their way to the United States in 1873 with the help of wealthy London silk merchant George Grant. Grant was bestowed thousands of acres of Kansas land from the Kansas and Pacific Railroad and settled the town of Victoria, Kansas. He imported four Angus bulls to improve the quality of beef produced by the native Longhorn cattle.

The popularity of Angus cattle in the United States was enhanced in part by the breed's outstanding accomplishments in the carcass contest at the International Livestock Exposition in Chicago. In competitions from 1900 thru 1975, when the show closed, straightbred Angus won all but three carcass championships; two of the other winners were Angus crossbreeds. The superior carcass quality of Angus cattle was widely known from these days forth.

Certified Angus Beef is quick to point out, however, that Certified Angus Beef is distinctly different from and superior to beef marketed under the "Black Angus" or "Angus" names. Certified Angus Beef is the only Angus-type beef program approved and monitored by the American Angus Association. Only when beef carries the official, registered trademark of Certified Angus Beef has it passed the rigorous standards that classify it as a superior product.

What's acceptable and unacceptable under Certified Angus Beef

The cows and calves on this estate in northern Virginia enjoy the early spring sunshine along with the dogwoods in full bloom. The calves, the result of artificial insemination, represent the genetic future of the Angus breed.

standards? Well, the process begins at the licensed packing plant, where incoming cattle are scrutinized. They must be predominantly black hided. That's because purebred Angus cattle have black hides. Yet, crossbred cattle with mostly black hides are still eligible. The cattle must have typical beef cattle conformation. Dairy cattle, on the other hand, tend to produce large, angular shaped

muscles. And there must be no hump on the neck of the cattle, which is to minimize the Brahman cattle influence. Research has shown that Brahman cattle tend to produce carcasses with more variation in tenderness of steaks and roasts. In other words, not just purebred Angus cattle are eligible for this program. Cattle of Angus heritage or Angus-type characteristics are also eligible (Typically 40 percent of the cattle entering a packing plant meet the above live cattle specifications and are eligible for further carcass evaluation by the USDA grading service.)

As the Angus-type cattle are processed, their carcasses are marked with a stamp to maintain their identity. Following processing, the carcasses are presented to the USDA grader, an impartial third-party who evaluates the identified carcasses for the following marbling, maturity and yield grade attributes:

1) Certified Angus Beef carcasses must have a modest or higher degree of marbling. Marbling, the small white flecks of fat finely interspersed throughout the lean, is the main contributor to beef flavor and juiciness

Carcasses from Angus-type cattle are evaluated by USDA graders for quality specifications which insure the end product's high palatability.

and must be distributed evenly throughout the meat to yield a flavorful, juicy cut of beef.

2) All Certified Angus Beef carcasses must be in the "A" (youngest) maturity range. The USDA classifies beef maturity into five categories, A through E, with A being the youngest (9 to 30 months, physiologically). The physiological age of cattle is closely associated with quality of beef, and the youngest cattle tend to produce beef that is superior in color, texture and firmness.

3) Certified Angus Beef carcasses must be yield grade three or leaner. USDA yield grades are determined by three major factors, including external fat cover, and range from one to five, with one being the leanest and five the fattest.

Certified Angus Beef carcasses have a fine to medium marbling e. Marbling texture influences uality of beef, particularly from Choice and Prime carcasses, , although they possess a suffi-quantity of marbling, sometimes a coarse marbling texture that ively influences the quality of

e above specifications are listed procedures in the USDA's ultural Marketing Service, Live-, Meat, Grain and Feed Division ng manual as Schedule G1. efore, all cattle evaluated for the ied Angus Beef Program also ve a G1 stamp prior to evalua-If all carcass specifications are he USDA grader stamps the car-"Accepted as Specified," and arcass is rolled with a Certified s Beef carcass roll parallel to SDA grade roll. At this point, ertified carcass becomes a -added product for the res-teur and the consumer.

approximately 25% of the s-type cattle evaluated by the A grader meet the stringent fied Angus Beef specifica- and are stamped with the epted as Specified" shield. (In-upper left.) The Certified s Beef carcass roll is then ed parallel to the USDA grade

ese strict specifications enable approximately one in four cattle fied as eligible for Certified s Beef carcass evaluation to be ed and merchandised as Cer-Angus Beef. In comparison, ap-mately nine out of every ten ally graded carcasses can ob- USDA Choice grade. ove all, the Certified Angus Beef insures that the product will be rior in taste, tenderness and juici-How does Certified Angus Beef d against mislabeling of the uct during the fabrication ss as well as insure the overall esomeness of the product? All dures at licensed Certified

Angus Beef packing plants and fabricating plants are overseen by the USDA Food Safety and Inspection Service (FSIS). It is the FSIS who employs federal meat inspectors. In addition, the Certified Angus Beef Program monitors all Certified Angus Beef sales and insures that the in-tegrity of the Certified Angus Beef trademark is maintained. It provides promotional material to licensed es-tablishments so that they, too, may promote Certified Angus Beef.

All packing plants, fabricators, processors and distributors must be licensed by the American Angus As-sociation to produce and market product under the Certified Angus Beef trademark. Likewise, res-taurants and retail establishments who desire to identify and promote the product must be licensed, thereby completing the important Certified Angus Beef monitoring program en-compassing "the packing plant to the dinner plate."

Selected regional distributors make up the Certified Angus Beef food ser-vice distributor family. Distributors are licensed based upon their ability to custom process and age beef to their client's specifications. All Cer-tified Angus Beef food service dis-tributors are center-of-the-plate red meats specialists who enjoy the chal-lenge and the rewards of marketing a value-added product like Certified Angus Beef. The distributors' sales representatives are adept at procur-ing high quality raw materials for chefs in the "white-tablecloth" res-taurant, hotel and club segment of the food service industry. Distributors can gain the exclusive rights to the Certified Angus Beef trademark in their respective geographical areas based upon their prior profes-sionalism and achievement in repre-senting Certified Angus Beef. And they have experienced dramatic growth from coast to coast.

The Certified Angus Beef market-ing specialist for one east coast firm said a reason for the company's suc-cess is that "we use Certified Angus Beef to headline our program. We carry an extensive product line, but Certified Angus Beef alone is a state-ment that we offer only the best in products to our customers. We will offer any cut of Certified Angus Beef the chef desires."

Across the country, on the west coast, another licensed Certified Angus Beef distributorship has seen a "phenomenal amount of growth in the Certified Angus Beef Program. We have one of the largest and most affluent markets in the country to ser-vice. The fine establishments in this market require a superior product and have come to rely on Certified Angus Beef to satisfy that demand. My clients know the value of maintaining a top quality reputation.

At licensed Certified Angus Beef food service dis-tributors, Certified Angus Beef may be ordered by subprimals or be custom processed into steaks by journeyman meat cutters according to restaurateurs' personal specifications.

The stringent specifications behind Certified Angus Beef insure against dining room complaints and help build the all-important repeat busi-ness needed for success. Everyone who tries Certified Angus Beef judges it superior - and that's good for everyone's bottom line."

The program has grown, thanks to a superior Certified Angus Beef product and to knowledgeable dis-tributors who want to meet the demands of the 21st century. They will place the beef not only in hotels and "white-tablecloth" restaurants but also in casual diners, school cafeterias and professional sports team training camps.

The challenge of the American Angus Association is to indentify still more cattle producing carcasses that meet Certified Angus Beef require-ments. It will also continue to work with cattle producers to breed cattle yielding carcasses of high quality and, at the same time, the leanness that is demanded by today's con-sumers.

Certified Angus Beef predicts the potential market for high quality beef to be 8 to 10 percent of the present U.S. fed beef production. While this figure is considerably larger than the amount of Certified Angus Beef produced today, we can all thank this credible program, based solidly upon such valued palatability traits and backed up by the most committed family of breeders, processors and distributors in the world, for having laid the foundation toward more con-sistently tender, juicy and flavorful beef.

Cooking to Perfection

A GUIDE TO BASIC BEEF PREPARATION

By James L. Miller, CEC

Crescent Metal Products, Inc.

As this chapter on basic beef preparation is read, we hope there will be many points of interest to tantalize the imagination.

When the various methods of cookery and their application to specific meat cuts are discussed, it is important to first take a look at the composition of beef and the effects of heat at various stages of cooking.

As a general rule, meat is recognized as the body tissues of animals that can be eaten as food. The cuts that will be discussed are muscle tissues that contract and cause some part of the animal to move.

When a beef carcass is analyzed, the approximate composition is 60 percent moisture, 18 percent protein and 22 percent fat, whereas the lean muscle tissue (i.e. closely trimmed steak) is about 75 percent moisture, 18 percent protein and 7 percent fat.

Muscle tissue is made up of long muscle fibers bound together by thin sheets of connective tissue. These bundles of fibers are called the "grain" of meat. Carving is done across the grain so that chewing is with the grain.

Connective tissue is made up of three basic proteins - collagen, elastin and reticulin. Of the three, collagen and reticulin are weakened by heat. They begin to dissolve at a temperature of 140 degrees Fahrenheit (F). Prior to the onset of dissolving, there is a shortening, or shrinkage, that takes place at 135 degrees F. It is important to realize that 135 degrees F - when shortening of the connective tissue takes place - is not the magical temperature level for shrinkage but only a phase. White connective tissue can also be broken down by acids in a marinade, but this does not hold true for the yellow elastin, which must be removed or mechanically broken down.

The muscle tissue, bound by the connective tissue, goes through stages of independent shrinkage. The initial contraction takes place from 104 to 122 degrees F and a more severe "toughening" in a second stage from 149 to 167 degrees F. By the time 170 degrees F is reached, the muscle fibers have shrunk as much as they are going to and literally crack.

The major effect of heat on protein is its influence on product yield. The protein itself is not lost but merely changed. During change, moisture is reduced. Remember, meat is 60 to 75 percent moisture. (The percentage will vary depending on the specific cut of meat.) The moisture that is held by the muscle tissues and connective tissues will be squeezed by the shortening of the strands of fibers.

A visual comparison would be the wringing out of a damp towel. When the towel is soaked it contains a high volume of water. Now, take the towel and twist it to wring it out. The towel is shortened, and its water content is reduced. Thus, the towel is not able to contain its original volume of water.

So, what happens to all this moisture when the meat is shrinking and cannot contain the original amount? With the range of temperatures and various methods of cooking, the cell walls will expand and, in many cases, literally burst.

You can experience this with a water balloon. If heated, the water will expand. When the balloon walls reach their limit of retention, the balloon will rupture.

If the surrounding environment is at 212 degrees F or above, water will evaporate and produce steam or humidity. When the moisture is released in enough volume to seep from the meat, it results in the drippage or "fond" found in pans using dry-heat cooking methods. The moisture will carry with it the remains of the ruptured cell walls, which are protein and other nutrients. This is why the "fond" is deglazed - to recapture the protein and resulting flavors of the evaporated moisture.

The same process occurs in moist heat cookery. When stock is made, natural protein and resulting flavors are released due to the forced destruction of cell tissues in the meat fibers and connective tissues attached to the bones.

The final component of meat that should be understood is fat. Fat tissue provides insulation and a reserve energy source for the animal. Fat also serves as a protective barrier, hindering bacteria growth with its minimal moisture content as well as protecting lean muscle from excessive shrinkage during cold storage of meat. It can provide approximately 22 percent of carcass weight.

Fat plays a major role in the methods of cooking and the quality level of the end product. The industry has termed intramuscular fat "marbling."

Fat provides a natural lubricant for the meat fibers it surrounds. When heat is applied and the fat renders within the meat, it flows between the fibers making them easier to pull apart. This ease of separation is what is known as "tenderness." The less lubricant available, the more work required to break down the tissues for human digestion. That is why chefs have resorted to larding, barding and oil marinades for lean meats.

Fat also has a role in meat flavor. When meat is chewed, flavor compounds stimulate the flow of saliva. The initial impression of moistness derived from a piece of meat is the actual moisture content of the product. When this is extracted, fat takes over to help provide saliva and continue the sensation of moistness.

In studying the analysis of meat tissue, see the role various components play. Their reaction to applied heat and their varying amounts in different cuts of beef dictate the cooking process.

Methods of Cooking:

The reasons for cooking meat are lo‐cal. Centuries ago, man learned that when meat was subjected to heat, the meat was more palatable. Today this practice is continued but with a better u‐derstanding of how various methods of cookery affect meat and make it more ‐cious.

Chefs strive for the all-important eye‐peal of their presentations. Coloration ‐ the meat and accompanying sauce, si‐ dishes and garnishes are vital. Additio‐ effort is needed to create food aroma a entice the sense of smell. Likewise, the sense of sound is activated by a sizzlin‐ steak at tableside, for example. To achieve these sensual results, various methods of preparation are at our dis‐ posal.

The selection of cooking method is d‐tated by the meat cuts involved. For ea‐ of review, cooking methods can be clas‐sified in three distinct categories:

> **A. Cooking with Fat**
> 1. Deep frying
> 2. Shallow frying (pan-fry)
> 3. Sautéing
>
> **B. Cooking by Moist Heat**
> 1. Braising
> 2. Steaming
> 3. Stewing
> 4. Boiling
> 5. Poaching
>
> **C. Cooking by Dry Heat**
> 1. Roasting (baking)
> 2. Griddling
> 3. Grilling (broiling)

Regardless of which cooking method i‐ utilized, inevitably there will be some loss in the nutritive value of the product. As the natural fluids are squeezed from the meat, they carry with them fat, soluble vitamins and minerals.

Some of the B vitamins will be lost with‐ water drippage, and vitamin A with rendered fat. Very high temperatures destroy some thiamine. Overall, cooking won't truly reduce the nutritional value of meat unless it is grossly overcooked. In some cooking methods, the nutrients are retrieved in the braising liquid and gravies made from drippings or broths which are then served to the customer.

Cooking with Fat:

This method of cookery utilizes some form of animal or vegetable fat to transfer heat to the product in lieu of direct meat contact. The cooking medium can be clarified butter, lard, vegetable oil, rendered animal fats, etc. Depending on the fat, high temperatures can be obtained to sear small portions of meat in relatively short periods of time. Whether you are deep frying, pan-frying or sauté‐ ing, the products are normally portioned for short-term exposure to the fat and tend to be cut from areas of the animal with limited connective tissue.

Since deep frying is more commonly util‐ ized in the preparation of poultry, seafood and vegetables, focus instead on the methods of pan-frying and sauteing. Unlike deep fat frying, where the product is completely submerged in cooking oil, pan-frying and sautéing utilize limited amounts of cooking fat.

Apprentices are often confused as to the difference between the two methods as they are both normally performed on the range top. To differentiate: Pan-frying uses a generous amount of oil in cooking,

the product is normally coated with
[br]eading or batter. On the other hand,
[saut]éing is performed in a sauteuse or
[...]oir with a minimum amount of fat. To
[saut]é, cook hot and fast with the
[pro]duct oftentimes dusted in flour. The fat
[is m]erely used to prevent sticking to the
surface.

[B]eef items that lend themselves to the
[saut]é method include medallions (from
[the] tenderloin) and steaks (from the loin or
[rib]. This preparation can be performed in
back of the house or at tableside. Of-
[tent]imes it is finished at tableside and
[us]ed to increase customer participation
[and] provide dining room marketing.

[W]hen sautéing, it is vital to quickly sear
[the] meat on both sides and remove it from
[the] pan prior to deglazing. Should you
[hap]pen to add a cooking liquor or stock
[to] the meat in the sauté pan, the meat
[will] braise and can toughen.

[N]ormally the portions are cut to
[av]erage weights of 4 ounces for medal-
[lion]s and 7 to 8 ounces for loin or rib
[ste]aks. For a rule of thumb, the cooking
[tim]e for these items on high heat would

Sautéing Guidelines

[R]are:	2 minutes per side
[M]edium-rare:	3 minutes per side
[M]edium:	4 minutes per side
[W]ell:	6 minutes per side

In checking for doneness, chefs often
[uti]lize the "firmness to touch" method,
[ac]hieved with practice and experience.
[To] compare with the human hand in an
[op]en, relaxed state, the large thumb
[m]uscle between the thumb and index
[fin]ger would represent rare; stretched and
[ta]ut is medium, and a tightly closed fist
[m]uscle is a well-done firmness.

Since the product is normally serving
[si]ze, the use of a pocket thermometer is
[no]t standard practice. But you may relate
[th]e firmness to internal temperatures of;
[1]30 degrees F for rare, 140 degrees F for
[m]edium-rare, 150 degrees F for medium-
[w]ell and 160 degrees F or higher for well-
[d]one.

This firmness, or doneness to be more
[p]recise, is a method of measuring the
[a]mount of protein coagulation that has
[ta]ken place. Coagulation refers to the
[c]ooked state and level of shortening by
[th]e muscle tissues, i.e. protein.

Cooking by Moist Heat:

Cooking with moist heat includes braising, steaming, stewing, boiling and poaching. When beef is used, the most
commonly practiced procedures are braising and stewing. The others are used
sometimes but not often. Boiled brisket of
beef is a well-accepted item and a very
cost effective entree. Meat cuts used in
moist cooking generally have a high
amount of connective tissue. They are
referred to as the "less tender cuts." They
originate from muscle areas that are heavily used in movement of the animal.
These would include parts of the fore-
quarter, i.e. chuck, plate and brisket, as
well as the flank, tip and round. These
cuts are familiar in moist cooking but are
also processed for ground meat.

Braising and stewing follow the same
procedure in preparation with the initial
browning of the product via pan-frying,
sautéing, searing or griddling. The
product is then placed into a liquid
medium of stock, wine, water or deglazed
pan broth to simmer and is covered. The
simmering of the dish is accomplished on
stove top or in a 300 to 325 degree F
oven. The goal is to provide for the meat
a liquid environment of 185 degrees F, at
which temperature there will be a
tenderization of the connective tissues.
The collagen will become gelatinous,
and the minor strands of elastin will become fully contracted. The result is meat
that has fully cooked, with the vitamins
and minerals captured in the broth. The
sauce or gravy will be rich in flavor and
nutrients and is often fortified by the use
of mirepoix in preparation.

Commonly, large beef cuts of rolled
chuck and round are used in preparation
of pot roast and sauerbraten. Similar cuts
are frequently used for cubed or swiss
steaks and stews. One thing to keep in
mind with the large roasts for braising is
that the chuck cut will have a larger
amount of collagen than the lean round
and, therefore, should be braised slower
and longer for an end product with good
gelatinization .

Stewing involves more liquid than does
braising. Where a braised item may have
one-third to one-half of the meat submerged, the stew is normally completely
immersed in the cooking liquid. The meat
is then cooked until "fork tender."

*Grilling provides intense flavor to beef, like the strip loin
steak at Babe's Steakhouse in Philadelphia.*

Cooking by Dry Heat:

Dry heat cooking commonly uses cuts
from the rib, short loin, sirloin and, in
some cases, round roasts. These high
quality cuts are comprised of muscle tissues that are used less in the movement
of the animal and have a lower percentage of connective tissue. They are considered to be more tender.

The most recognized dry heat method is
roasting or baking large, primal cuts. Griddling, broiling and grilling also use dry
heat because there is no introduction of
fat or liquid during the cooking process.
Griddling involves the use of a hot, flat surface which should be 400 degrees F for
meats. No oil is added to the surface -
the rendered fat from the meat prevents
sticking. Pan-broiling is another form of
griddling, as is the use of the flat top or
"French top" area of the stove.

Braising Guidelines

Pot Roast	3 to 5 pounds	2 to 3 hours
Sauerbraten	3 to 5 pounds	2 to 3 hours
Stew, 1-inch cubes		1 to 1 1/2 hours
Stew, 2-inch cubes		1 1/2 to 2 hours
Short ribs	8 ounces	1 1/2 to 2 hours

Note: These cooking times are based on simmering time after the broth is brought to
a boil and heat is reduced.

Use the "firmness to touch" method to gauge a steak's doneness.

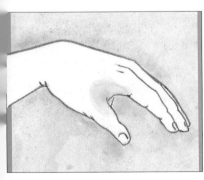

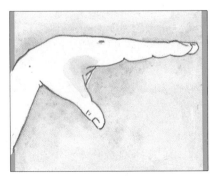

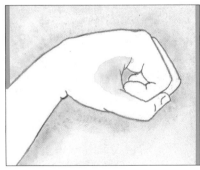

Rare - *The human hand is in an open,
relaxed state. Press the large thumb
muscle between thumb and index finger,
and it will feel like rare steak.*

Medium - *Stretch out your hand. Press
the same muscle and it will feel like steak
cooked to medium doneness.*

Well-done - *Clench a tight fist, and the
thumb muscle will feel like well-done
steak.*

The famous "Pittsburgh-style" steak is produced by griddling. The steak is charred on the outside and still blue in the center. Small rib steaks and loin steaks for breakfast and lunch service are invariably cooked by griddling.

Unlike the relatively low temperature used for griddling, grilling and broiling utilize extremely high temperatures, generated from below the food product

Prime rib, such as the one prepared by Thomas Catherall of Cherokee Town & Country Club in Atlanta, may be cooked by traditional roasting or a slow-roasting method.

during grilling and above the product in the case of broiling. The heat source may be a gas flame, charcoal, wood or an electrical broiling element. Because the temperature of a gas flame is 3000 degrees F and an electrical element is 2000 degrees F, it is imperative that single serving pieces of meat be used with grilling or broiling. The interior must be cooked before the exterior is burned.

Grilling or broiling is cooking by direct, radiant heat. By the time the heat radiates through a few inches of air, the temperature will vary from 350 to 550 degrees F. Chefs can regulate the cooking speed by adjusting the proximity of the heat source to the meat. This heated air provides a natural convection.

Grilled or broiled items are popular because of the intense flavor produced by surface browning. Since there are normally no additional oils and fats used, grilling and broiling are highly touted as being healthful cooking methods. Care must be exercised to prevent fat from burning.

When grilling, the fat may be scored so the steak doesn't curl, and you may add flavor to the meat by briefly marinating before cooking or adding a flavored butter after cooking.

In the roasting of beef, a dry environment is used. This promotes the browning of surface tissues and the resulting flavor associated with roasting.

While there are many methods of roasting, some basic procedures should be followed: The roast should always be placed on a rack and not allowed to rest flush on the bottom of the pan. Escaped fluids and rendered fats will create simmering, and instead of roasting, the meat will braise in these liquids. Roast fat side up so that the meat can baste itself in its own fat. Never add water to the pan or cover the pan. This will result in steaming, not roasting, and produce a much different end product.

How chefs season roasts is up to them, but keep in mind that the flavors from salt, pepper and herbs will penetrate no more than 1/4 to 1/2 inch into the meat. The interior remains untouched unless needle marination is used.

Some roasts that are prepared with the bones intact will require less cooking time than the same cut prepared boneless. For example, the "export" rib roast involves a Meat Buyer's Guide (MBG) No. 109 rib cut with the fat cap and chine bones removed. The rib bones left in place expedite cooking time by transferring heat and by allowing heated air to flow beneath their natural bridge. If you place this roast side by side with a No. 112A rib eye in the oven at the same temperature, you will find the export rib needs less cooking time.

Once meats have been cooked by roasting, they need time for resting, called the set-up time. At 5 to 10 degrees below the desired internal temperature, remove the roast from the oven. This allows juices to redistribute, water-retaining tissues to relax and carving to be much easier. Use a sharp knife when carving because a dull knife will actually saw the meat and create unnecessary fluid loss.

Standard roasting involves the preheating of an oven to temperatures of 300 to 350 degrees F. The meat is prepared and then placed in the hot oven. Using an accurate meat thermometer, the roast is pulled from the oven at 5 to 10 degrees prior to the finished internal temperature and allowed to rest for 15 to 20 minutes prior to carving. An option to this is to turn the oven off when the roast reaches an internal temperature of 115 to 120 degrees F and allow the meat to finish cooking, set up and rest as the oven cools.

While there are as many meat roasting charts, time and temperature tables and written programs for roasting guides as there are cookbooks, below is a basic time and temperature table for beef cooked medium-rare.

An accurate way to gauge the correct temperature for roasting would be to use stem or digital probe thermometer. It m be placed in the muscle only. Fat and b will give a higher reading than lean mus tissue. Remember, you should take a r from the oven when the thermometer re 5 to 10 degrees short of the desired temperature. Therefore, when the thermometer shows 130 degrees F the roas should be removed from the oven to produce a rare degree of finished donen (remove at 140 degrees F for medium a 160 degrees F for well-done).

Although the concept of a chef "sealin the juices inside to prohibit their release been proven a falsehood, the high heat searing method of roasting dates back many centuries. The exterior of the mea "barked," or heavily browned, by the use 450 to 475 degrees F for about 15 minut Then the oven is lowered in temperature 250 to 300 degrees F to finish the proces The meat is removed from the oven and lowed to set-up, or rest, as in standard roasting.

Since the exterior is not waterproof, thi high heat treatment allows for additional shrinkage through further evaporation of moisture from within the meat. Many chef prefer this method but pay in yield loss fo the intense flavor of the crust and resultin au jus. There are some cuts of beef that are ideal for this method of searing and finishing. The chateaubriand or tenderloir is excellent when prepared in this fashion as is the British forerib. Their small sizes make them well-adapted to this procedure.

Swift and Company, many years ago, published an article on what they termed "Delayed Cooking." This was similar to the high heat/two stage method. They took a pound rib roast and browned it for 1 1/2 hours at 350 degrees F, then turned the oven down to 140 degrees F for 3 1/2 hou to attain the 140 degrees F internal tempe ture. The key to the process was the use o extremely accurate temperature control of within 5 degrees F, plus or minus. Many c sider this the first step toward our third roa ing method of low-temperature roasting.

The slow roasting or low-temperature preparation of meats has become one of the most common methods practiced in meat cookery. With a clearer understandin of meat's reaction to heat and the relativel high cost of the practice of dry aging, the ir dustry has recognized this method as one to provide a quality end product in an affor dable manner. Low-temperature roasting i practiced at levels of 210 to 250 degrees F with gentle heating to minimize yield loss. Minimal shrinkage in tender, flavorful roast: can be achieved with specially designed equipment.

Manufacturers of slow-roast ovens do have slow convected air models available that provide browning, or "Maillard Reaction." This "Maillard Reaction" was discovered in 1912 and is the browning of the surface of meat in dry heat conditions, due to the presence of amino acids and sugars in the meat, and begins at 194 degrees F. Slow-cooking ovens are fully automatic with a holding cycle to promote set-up, carry-over cooking and, most omportantly, enzyme action to tenderize the meat. The enzyme action is identical to the aging process but performed at an increased rate due to controlled, higher temperature levels of the holding cycle.

Additional equipment for controlled, low-temperature roasting, or more properly termed combination cooking, have entered our kitchens. The various models of combination convection/steam ovens provide the use of dry and moist cooking for flavor, browning and improved yield. Both the combi-ovens and roast-and-hold ovens offer probe systems for accurate roasting doneness. Follow manufacturers' recommended cooking procedures for meat preparation, and remember a chef can always make adjustments to suit his/her level of expectation.

Roasting Guidelines

Cut of Beef	Oven Temperature	Time
Standing rib roast	325 degrees F	20 min. per lb.
Tenderloin roast (4-6 lbs.)	450 degrees F	approx. 30 min. total

Guidelines for Broiling and Grilling

Loin steak	2-inch thickness	Rare	4 minutes per side
		Medium-rare	5 1/2-6 minutes per side
		Medium	8 minutes per side
Tenderloin	3-inch thickness	Rare	4 minutes per side
		Medium-rare	5 minutes per side
		Medium	7 minutes per side
Porterhouse, T-bone	1-inch thickness	Rare	3 minutes per side
		Medium-rare	4 1/2 minutes per side
		Medium	6 minutes per side
Hamburger	2-inch thickness	Medium-rare	4 minutes per side
		Medium	6 minutes per side

Note: Times will vary with the equipment used and the initial temperature of the meat.

Chatham Bars Inn Chatham, Massachusetts

ROLAND CZEKELIUS

Roland Czekelius is executive chef at a Cape Cod resort called Chatham Bars Inn, but he might as well be a salesman for Certified Angus Beef.

That's because Czekelius prepares an exclusive line-up of Certified Angus Beef products, from strip steak to tenderloin, ribs, ground beef for hamburgers, flanks, to even cubed meat for goulash. "I'm sold," said Czekelius, who doesn't just write "beef" on the menu but instead lists "Certified Angus Beef."

"I know the guests can tell a difference in this beef, and I for one can tell you there is a big difference between this beef and ordinary beef," the chef said.

Czekelius made the move from his executive chef's job at the 1,000-room Bos-

ton Park Plaza to this landmark ocean-front resort a little more than a year ago. He and his wife were ready to get out of crowded Boston, and the Cape seemed a fitting locale for the chef, whose family in Austria had owned a 42-room inn.

Born and raised in Tyrol, Austria, Czekelius apprenticed at the Schloss Hotel near Innsbruck, but recalls it was his 11 months in military service in northern Italy that affected the way he cooks today. The impressionable young chef was introduced to northern Italian cooking, something he cannot get out of his system.

While he has worked in Holland, Jerusalem, and on a cruise line that sailed to Bermuda and the Caribbean, Czekelius is at home in New England. He likes the climate, and eagerly awaits the chance to ski each winter. He was a member of the Austrian national ski team about the time he learned to cook.

Most recently, Czekelius was captain of the New England culinary team at the 1988 Culinary Olympics in Frankfurt.

Rolled Flank Steak with Sesame Crust

Recipe on page 19

RAGOUT OF BEEF WITH WILD MUSHROOMS AND DRIED FRUITS

(Serves 6)

For the marinade:
1 1/2 cups good red wine
    (Bordeaux or Beaujolais)
1 1/4 cups water
3 medium-size shallots, sliced
1 cup sliced carrots
1/2 cup diced celery
3 garlic cloves, minced
1 bay leaf
3 cloves
10 peppercorns
1 teaspoon sugar
1 tablespoon salt

For the garnish:
Fresh chives

For the beef:
2 1/2 pounds Certified Angus
    Beef stew meat (chuck)
3/4 cup dried fruits (prunes, apples,
    apricots, pears, raisins)
2 cups tea
Orange and lemon peel
3/4 cup whole cloves
1 cinnamon stick
2 tablespoons olive oil
1 1/4 cups mushrooms (cèpes,
    shiitakes, chanterelles)
1 tablespoon tomato paste
2 cups red wine (Chianti or Burgundy)
1-2 slices pumpernickel bread,
    crumbled
1/2 cup heavy cream
Salt and pepper to taste

For the marinade, combine all ingredients.

For the beef, marinate the meat three days in advance. The meat should be cleaned, all excess fat removed and cut into 1-inch dice or any size you desire. Soak dried fruits in tea with lemon and orange peel, cloves and cinnamon overnight.

Strain marinade through a china cap. Remove meat, dry with kitchen towel, and set aside. Bring marinade to a boil, skimming off the foam with a ladle and discard. Heat oil in a heavy sauté or roast pan. Quickly roast meat evenly on all sides. Add the mushrooms and sauté until all the water from the mushrooms has evaporated. Stir in the tomato paste. Deglaze with the red wine, add the marinade, bring to a boil, close pan with lid and place in oven at 375 degrees F. Allow to cook for a 1/2 hour, then sprinkle in the pumpernickel crumbs. Continue cooking for 1 hour.

Remove meat from the stew and keep warm. Puree and strain the sauce. Add the cream. Cut the dried fruits into assorted shapes and add to the sauce along with the meat and slowly cook for 5 minutes. Season to taste with salt and pepper and serve.

OT-AU-FEU WITH SEMOLINA QUENELLES

(ves 4)

For the broth:
1 1/2 pounds beef bones
1 pound beef trimmings
3 cups diced onions
1 bouquet garni
3 1/2 tablespoons diced smoked
 bacon
3 1/2 tablespoons tomato paste
1 teaspoon juniper berries
1/2 teaspoon black peppercorns
3 bay leaves
1/2 bottle Beaujolais
1/2 cup baby turnips
1 carrot
2 leeks
1 cup small chanterelles
1/2 cup shiitake mushrooms
2 small, sweet onions
1/2 cup tiny French beans
1 1/4 pounds Certified Angus Beef
 tenderloin (head end)
Salt and fresh ground pepper

For the semolina quenelles:
4 tablespoons butter, softened
Salt and nutmeg to taste
1 egg
1 cup semolina flour

For the garnish:
Fresh thyme and marjoram

For the semolina quenelles, beat the soft butter and salt until foamy. Add the nutmeg. Mix in the egg and add the semolina. Let cool in refrigerator for 1 hour. Mound quenelles with teaspoon and cook in lightly salted water for 10 minutes. Let sit for another 5 minutes and serve.

For the stock, place chopped bones and beef trimmings in roasting pan. Add diced onions, bouquet garni and diced bacon. Mix in the tomato paste and add juniper berries, peppercorns, bay leaves and Beaujolais. Roast at 450 degrees F for about 40-50 minutes. (Stir once in awhile to avoid burning.) After roasting, place all ingredients in large pot and add one gallon of cold water and bring slowly to a boil. Continue to boil over moderate heat for 3-4 hours. (It will reduce to 1/2 of the original amount.) While your stock is boiling, clean all other vegetables. Cut into different shapes and styles. Remove silver skin from tenderloin and place in the broth. Allow to simmer for 12 minutes.

Arrange all vegetables and quenelles in a soup terrine, remove tenderloin, slice on a diagonal in 1/2-inch thin slices, salt both sides and arrange in center of soup terrine. Carefully ladle broth into soup terrine, and serve.

13

LARRY FORGIONE

An American Place
New York,
New York

Larry Forgione's menu at An American Place in Manhattan reads right out of a Rand McNally atlas: Chesapeake Bay Deviled Crab, Fresh Florida Key West Shrimp, California Endive, Fried New England Ipswich Clams, Warm Michigan Baby White Asparagus Plate, New York Steak Sandwich Philly Style.

It's no wonder because Forgione, longtime friend and mentor of the late James Beard and 1974 graduate of the Culinary Institute of America, goes to great lengths to prepare foods made in the U.S.A. His convivial bistro, An American Place at Park Avenue and 32nd Street, with its maize-colored walls, deep wood tones and Art Deco touches, is one of the more highly praised restaurants in New York City. And Forgione has been called the modern day Father of American Cuisine. "I do feel I was instrumental in the movement to familiarize American products and foods, and to establish our past and present relationships with them," Forgione said, modestly. "But

as for titles, well, I'll leave that up to food journalists.

"I cook with all-American ingredients for very positive reasons. This started when I was at the River Cafe. I made the statement that I could create wonderful food with just what America has to offer . . . what I meant was that I could cook without European truffles and foie gras, even though now these

products are made right here in the United States," Forgione said.

Certified Angus Beef is one American product that Forgione high touts, and he prepares the filet and strip steak at An American Place. "Over the years people have talked about the non-popularity of beef," he said. "That may be true for the home, but when people go out to eat they want to eat beef." Dining at Forgione's restaurant is much like coming home. Portions are ample, ingredients have taste and the food is as down to earth as the chef's gentle personality. A likeable and accomplished man, Forgione has received his share of honors: CIA's 1987 Chef of the Year, 1988 IVY Award Winner by Restaurant and Institutions Magazine and included in th Who's Who in American Cooking by Cook's Magazine in 1984.

When he's not in his restaurant, Forgione is working with American Spoon Foods in Petoskey, Michigan; he is co-owner of the company that specializes in custom preserves, sauces and condiments. He is also active in charity work and has been instrumental in the American Chefs Tribute to James Beard, which has raised millions of dollars for Citymeals-on-Wheels in New York City.

CHARRED FILET OF BEEF WITH CHILI CORN SAUCE

(Serves 4)

For the sauce:

2 tablespoons vegetable oil
Beef trimmings
1 onion, sliced
1 tablespoon finely chopped garlic
1 red pepper, finely chopped,
 trimming reserved
1 green pepper, finely chopped,
 trimming reserved
2 1/2 tablespoons chili powder
1/4 teaspoon cayenne pepper
1/4 teaspoon freshly ground black
 pepper
2 tablespoons dry white wine
1 1/2 cups veal or beef stock
1 cup heavy cream
1 cup corn kernels, preferably freshly
 shucked

For the beef:

4 6-8 ounce Certified Angus Beef
 filets with trimmings
Salt and freshly ground black pepper
 to taste
1 tablespoon vegetable oil

For the sauce, heat the oil in a heavy sauté pan over medium high heat until very hot. Brown the beef trimmings in the oil. Add the sliced onion to the pan and cook until lightly browned. Add the garlic and the pepper trimmings. Cook the mixture for another minute. Turn the contents of the pan into a strainer to remove excess oil. Return vegetables to the pan and stir in the chili powder, cayenne, and pepper.

Lower the heat and cook, stirring, for 2 to 3 minutes. Add the wine and stir briefly, scraping the bottom and sides of the pan. Add the stock to the pan. Raise the heat to high and bring the mixture to a boil, skimming any fat or foam off the surface. Cook for 7 to 8 minutes until the mixture is reduced by about half and has a syrupy consistency. Put the cream in a 1-quart saucepan and simmer for about 5 minutes, until thickened, skimming off any foam. Strain the reduced chili mixture into the cream and whisk to blend. Stir in the red and green peppers and the corn and simmer for 3 to 4 minutes, until the corn is tender. If the sauce begins to separate or curdle, strain it into a blender, add a few tablespoons of heavy cream and blend just until smooth.

For the beef, season the steaks with salt and pepper. Heat the oil in a cast iron skillet or heavy sauté pan until very hot. Add the steaks and char evenly for 3 to 4 minutes on each side for medium-rare.

AN AMERICAN PLACE "PHILLY CHEESESTEAK"

(Serves 6)

For the Philly cheesesteak:
2 tablespoons peanut oil
6 4-5 ounce Certified Angus Beef
   strip loin steaks, trimmed of all fat
Salt and fresh ground pepper to taste
6 hero-size loaves of Dutch potato
   buns
1 onion, sliced very thin
1 red bell pepper, seeded and sliced
   very thin
1 green bell pepper, seeded and
   sliced very thin
1 jalapeño pepper, seeded and
   chopped very fine
12 slices aged Crowley, colby or
   white cheddar cheese, sliced 1/8-
   inch thick
1 1/2 cups beef broth

For the Dutch potato bread:
1 large potato
1 1/2 cups water
1 package active dry yeast
1/4 teaspoon sugar
1/2 cup buttermilk
1/2 tablespoon salt
3 to 4 cups all-purpose flour
1 egg yolk
2 tablespoons water

For the garnish:
Fresh hot potato chips
Small green salad

For the Dutch potato bread, peel the
potato and cut into small pieces. Place in
a saucepan and add 1 1/2 cups of water.
Bring to a boil and cook until the potato is
soft. Drain the potatoes reserving the li-
uid. (You should have approximately 3,
cup of potato liquid). Mash the potato u
smooth and set aside. Measure out 1/2
cup of potato water and let cool to 110-
115 degrees F in a small bowl. Add the
yeast and sugar and stir to dissolve the
yeast. Let stand until foamy (approxima
ly 10-12 minutes). Warm the buttermilk
a saucepan, remove from the heat and
add the mashed potatoes and salt. Stir
making sure the potatoes are smooth.
Add the yeast mixture. Add 1/2 of the
flour. With a wooden spoon vigorously s
until a soft dough is formed. Turn out o
a lightly floured surface and knead for
about 7-8 minutes, adding dusting of flc
if needed. The dough should be soft an
moist, not dry. Place in a lightly oiled bo
turning once or twice to evenly coat the
dough. Cover and let rise to double in
volume in a warm place (approximately
45 minutes to 1 hour). Punch down the
. dough and turn out onto a lig
ly floured surface.

*continue
on page*

RILLED SIRLOIN STEAK MARINATED WITH BEER

ves 4)

For the marinade:
12 ounces amber beer
1 1/2 cups chicken or veal stock
1/2 teaspoon fresh thyme leaves
1 cup peeled, seeded and chopped
 tomatoes
1 teaspoon Worcestershire sauce
5 drops Tabasco sauce
1 bay leaf
1/2 teaspoon freshly ground black
 pepper
1/2 teaspoon salt
1/4 cup chopped parsley

For the beef:
4 Certified Angus Beef top sirloin butt
 steaks or 1 1/4 pounds flank steak
Vegetable oil
Salt and freshly ground black pepper
 to taste
8 tablespoons (1 stick) unsalted
 butter, at room temperature, cut into
 small pieces

For the garnish:
Grilled leeks

For the marinade, combine all the ingredients in a glass or porcelain dish large enough to hold the meat in a single layer and mix thoroughly. Place the steaks in the marinade, cover, and let them sit for 4 to 12 hours in the refrigerator. Turn the meat from time to time.

For the beef, prepare a charcoal fire. Remove the steaks from the marinade and pat dry. Rub the meat with a little oil and season with salt and pepper. Pour the marinade into a saucepan and bring to a boil, skimming off any foam that rises to the surface.

continued on page 19

GRILLED T-BONE STEAK WITH MISSOURI STYLE MOREL FRIES

Larry Forgione

(Serves 4)

For the sauce:
1 teaspoon vegetable oil
1 onion, sliced
1 teaspoon minced garlic
2 tablespoons tomato puree
2 tablespoons cider vinegar
1 teaspoon sugar
2 cups beef stock
2 tablespoons butter

For the beef:
Peanut oil for frying
4 18-ounce Certified Angus Beef
 T-bone steaks
2 tablespoons vegetable oil
Salt and freshly ground black pepper
 to taste
1/2 pound fresh morels, trimmed
 and cut in half lengthwise
1 cup half and half
1 cup all-purpose flour
1/2 cup stone-ground cornmeal
1 teaspoon salt
1/2 teaspoon ground black pepper
1/2 teaspoon cayenne pepper

For the sauce, in a heavy skillet, hea
the oil and sauté the onion until lightly
browned. Add the garlic and tomato pur
and continue to cook for another 2
minutes. Add the vinegar and sugar and
cook for another minute or two. Add the
beef stock, bring to a boil and skim the s
face of any oil. Lower the heat and redu
to thicken by half. Remove from the fire
and stir in the butter. Strain and set asic
Keep warm.

For the beef, preheat peanut oil in fry
or frying pot to 375 degrees. Prepare a
moderately hot charcoal fire. Rub the
steaks with the oil and season with salt
and the freshly ground black pepper. Gr
the steaks over the fire for 4-5 minutes p
side for medium-rare.

continued on next pag

LED FLANK STEAK WITH SAME CRUST

and
kelius

page 11

es 4)

For the garnish:
Mushroom risotto
Fresh herbs

For the flank steak:
1 1/2 pounds Certified Angus Beef
  flank steak
Salt and pepper to taste
2 ounces zucchini
2 ounces eggplant
2 ounces summer squash
2 ounces red and yellow pepper
1/2 cup plus 1 tablespoon olive oil
Dijon mustard
Sesame seeds

For the sauce:
1 1/4 pounds fresh tomatoes
3 tablespoons minced shallots
2 tablespoons butter
1/3 cup olive oil
1 garlic clove, pureed
Salt and sugar to taste
15 fresh basil leaves

For the sauce, peel tomatoes and cut into small dice. Saute the shallots in butter and olive oil with the tomatoes. Add the pureed garlic clove, salt and sugar, and simmer for 15 minutes. Julienne the fresh basil, and add before serving.

For the beef, clean flank steak, remove veins and excess fat. Lay on plastic wrap and sprinkle with salt and pepper. Clean all the vegetables and cut in long thin strips. Season with salt and pepper. Dip in olive oil. Grill slices on very hot grill for a short time. Dry on a paper towel and arrange the vegetable slices in the center of the steak. Roll flank steak, keeping vegetables in center. Tie with butcher string. Heat olive oil in a skillet, and when hot, sear meat on all sides until brown. Place in preheated oven at 350 degrees F for about 20 minutes. Remove, rub with Dijon mustard and roll in sesame seeds. Return to oven until sesame seeds brown. Slice and arrange on plate with tomato sauce, mushroom risotto and fresh herbs.

AMERICAN PLACE "PHILLY CHEESESTEAK"

wrence
rgione

m page 16

Divide into 6 even pieces. Form into hero-shaped loaves and place on a baking sheet with any seams on the bottom. Cover the tray and let rise again for

30 minutes. Gently brush the tops with the egg yolk and water mixture. Bake in a preheated 375 degree oven for 30 minutes or until the loaves are golden brown and crisp. Set the loaves on a rack to cool.

For the Philly cheesesteak, preheat broiler or salamander. In a large heavy skillet, heat the 2 tablespoons of oil until quite hot. With a mallet, flatten the steaks slightly and season with salt and fresh ground black pepper. Split each of the buns in half lengthwise and set on a cookie sheet or pan. Add the steaks to the skillet and cook on both sides for 2-3 minutes. Repeat the procedure until all the steaks are cooked. As the steaks cook, place each down on the bottom half of the buns. Add the onions, peppers and jalapeño to the skillet after the last steak is

cooked. Stir continuously until the onions are evenly cooked. With a spoon evenly distribute the sauteed onions and peppers on top of each steak. Lay two slices of cheese over each steak and place the tray under your preheated broiler until the cheese melts completely. While the cheese is melting, add the 1 1/2 cups of broth to the skillet in which the steaks and peppers were cooked. Bring to a boil Strain into a small saucepan. When the cheese is completely melted remove the sandwiches from the broiler and place on a cutting board. Drizzle the inside of the top half of each bun with a few tablespoons of the broth and place on top of each steak. Cut the sandwiches in half and serve with a ramekin of the beef broth for dipping.

For the garnish, serve with fresh hot potato chips and a small salad.

RILLED SIRLOIN STEAK MARINATED WITH BEER

awrence
orgione

om page 17

Lower the heat and simmer until the marinade is reduced by about half, 15 to 20 minutes. Continue to skim off any fat that rises as the marinade reduces. Remove the bay leaf from the marinade and stir in the butter, a piece at a time, making sure one piece is incorporated into the mixture before adding the next. Keep

warm until ready to serve. Grill the steaks over the hot charcoal fire for 3 to 4 minutes per side for medium-rare. Remove the steaks from the grill, spoon over the reduced marinade and serve immediately.

For garnish, grill sliced leeks and serve with steaks.

GRILLED T-BONE STEAK WITH MISSOURI STYLE MOREL FRIES

awrence
orgione

rom page 18

While the steaks are cooking, place the morels in a bowl and pour over the light cream and toss. In a second bowl, combine the flour, cornmeal, salt, pepper and cayenne and stir to evenly distribute the spices. Drain the morels and add to the flour mixture, tossing to evenly coat the morels. Place the morels in frying bas-

kets. Do not overcrowd the mushrooms. Fry until golden brown. Drain the mushrooms into an absorbent cloth and season lightly with salt. Repeat the procedure until all the morels are fried.

To serve, place the grilled steaks with the steak sauce on plates and garnish with crispy fried morels.

ANDRÉ SOLTNER

Lutèce
New York,
New York

To dine at least once at Lutèce is on just about everyone's wish list. That's because the restaurant on East 50th Street in Manhattan is the most respected and serious French restaurant on this side of the Atlantic Ocean.

André Soltner is Lutèce's lifeline, chef and proprietor, made possible by Soltner spending his every waking hour at the restaurant. He virtually lives here, three floors above in his townhouse with his wife and maître'd Simone.

"Every restaurant needs a good woman, and this is Simone," Soltner said. "She doesn't interfere with my cooking and is in charge of the reception and is cashier... we never disagree in the restaurant, but we might fight behind closed doors just like any married couple."

Unlike other chefs who bask in the celebrity spotlight and donate their energies to fund-raising dinners around the country, Soltner is a homebody. He budges only from Lutèce to spend Sundays in the Catskill mountains where the couple has a second home. And for several weeks in August he travels back to his French homeland - to Alsace if he has his way, to Normandy if his wife chooses, and to Paris if it's a joint decision.

Born and raised the son of a cabinet-maker in Alsace, André Soltner worked in hotels in France and Switzerland before joining the French military at 21 years of age. But it was when he was sous chef and then executive chef at the Parisian restaurant Chez Hansi, that he was spotted by André Surmain and asked in 1961 to open Surmain's New York restaurant called Lutèce. Soltner became the sole owner of Lutèce in 1973.

In 28 years he has built a phenomenal success story, the recipient of numerous French culinary honors. Soltner was presented with the highest award for craftsmen, the Meilleur Ouvrier de France in 1968. And he was named Chef of the Year in 1986 by the Culinary Institute of America.

His customers vie for precious reservations with as much determination as they might highly acclaimed Broadway performances. But Soltner is sure to turn down more would-be patrons than the box offices. Tickets to Lutèce go on sale one month in advance, and a Saturday night will sell out in an hour. Soltner estimates for every reservation he accepts, he turns 30 away.

"I feel terrible. Everyone thinks it would be great to be this successful, but for me it's a problem. We are in the business to please people, and this way we cannot," Soltner said.

And the thought of expanding rubs against his grain. "If you expand you have to move and I wouldn't want to do that. You'd need a manager and a bigger staff, and people would then say it's not what it used to be," Soltner said.

Invariably the question of retiring comes up in a conversation with Soltner, who is 56. There's no way he'd leave the cooking profession entirely, he said. What he'd like to do is teach.

"Teaching students to cook is really my dream. Not because I need the money, but because I have so much to share," he said.

"BAECKEOFE"

(Serves 8)

For the meat:

1 pound Certified Angus Beef brisket, trimmed

2 pigs feet

1 pound lamb shoulder

1 pound pork shoulder

For the marinade:

2 1/4 cups Alsatian white wine

1 cup chopped onions

2 cloves garlic, minced

1 bouquet garni of parsley, thyme and bay leaf

Pepper

To assemble:

2 pounds potatoes, peeled and sliced

2 medium onions, thinly sliced

Alsatian wine to moisten

Salt and pepper to taste

For the pastry top:

1 cup all-purpose flour

4 to 5 tablespoons water

For the meat, cut the beef, pigs feet, lamb and pork into equal pieces, about 1 inch in size.

For the marinade, combine wine, onions, garlic, bouquet garni and pepper. Marinate meat in this mixture for 24 hours.

To assemble, remove meat from marinade. In a pottery baking dish with lid, place half of the sliced potatoes, then meat, then onions, then another layer of potatoes. Wet with Alsatian wine and season with salt and pepper. Cover dish and seal around edges with pastry dough made from combining flour with water. Bake at 300 degrees F for 2 1/2 hours.

To serve, remove pastry crust, open lid and spoon out onto plates. Garnish with fresh herbs, if desired.

TENDERLOIN OF BEEF IN BRIOCHE

(Serves 8)

For the Beef:
1 5-pound Certified Angus Beef
  tenderloin
2 pounds mushrooms, chopped
6 shallots, minced
2 tablespoons butter
8 ounces foie gras, cut into little cubes
Salt and pepper to taste
1 tablespoon minced parsley
1 pound brioche dough
Beaten egg

To serve:
Madeira sauce to which finely
  chopped truffles have been added

For the brioche dough:
1/3 ounce fresh yeast or 1 package
  active dry yeast
2 tablespoons warm water
  (110 degrees F)
2 1/4 cups flour (half cake flour,
  half bread flour)
1 1/2 teaspoons salt
2 tablespoons sugar
3 to 4 medium eggs
6 1/4 ounces soft butter

For the beef, trim tenderloin and tie with string to keep it in shape. Roast in a buttered pan in a 450 degree F oven for 12 minutes, basting it and turning it to brown on all sides. Remove from oven to cool.

Cook mushrooms and shallots in butter. Add foie gras and salt and pepper to taste. Add parsley. Let cool.

Roll brioche dough into a rectangle 1/4-inch thick and large enough to envelop the filet. Lay filet in center and coat it with mushroom mixture. Wrap filet in brioche. Turn seams under and brush all over with beaten egg.

Let brioche rise for 45 minutes at room temperature. Bake in a 350 degree oven for 25 minutes or until pastry is nicely browned.

To serve, slice and place on a pool of Madeira sauce.

For the brioche dough, place yeast in bottom of a mixing bowl and add water. Stir to dissolve. Add flour, salt and sugar. With dough hook fitted in electric mixer begin mixing. Add 3 eggs and soft butter. Mix about 6 to 8 minutes or until dough pulls away from the sides of the bowl. Add extra egg, if needed, during mixing. Cover bowl with a wet, clean kitchen towel and place in refrigerator for 2 to 3 hours. Punch dough down and knead for 1 minute.

Le Bec Fin
Philadelphia,
Pennsylvania

GEORGES PERRIER

Like so many Frenchmen, Georges Perrier was a young man when he began cooking, apprenticing and then working in French kitchens. But the native of Lyon, in the heart of Burgundy, did at an early age what many Frenchmen are now only contemplating - he came to the United States.

At 23 years of age, he cooked in the kitchen of La Panetiere in Philadelphia. And at that time - 1967 - Philadelphia, like so many U.S. cities, was without the wealth of ingredients it has today. The pickings were certainly slim for this French chef accustomed to fresh herbs, specialty produce and fresh seafood.

Perrier, who has lived half his life in the United States, has said he initially relied on his mother to transport (smuggle)

necessary ingredients, such as foie gra from France into Philadelphia.

But the raw ingredients have caught with the talent. Philadelphia provisions bountiful, and Perrier, chef/ proprietor Le Bec Fin since 1970, has little trouble finding what ingredients he needs. Tha cludes beef, and he selects Certified Angus Beef.

At Le Bec Fin, Perrier and his staff o work dinners and produce from 90 to 1 covers nightly. The restaurant has continued to be the finest French restaurar in Philadelphia and one of the best in th country.

Perrier was recently named 1989 Ch of the Year by the Maîtres Cuisiniers de France and the Academie Culinaire de France.

SMOKED SIRLOIN WITH WATERCRESS SAUCE

(Serves 2)

For the sirloin steak:
1 1- pound Certified Angus Beef
  strip loin
1 tablespoon salt
1 tablespoon ground white pepper
1 tablespoon crushed peppercorns

For the watercress sauce:
1 bunch watercress
1/2 cup chervil
1/4 teaspoon Dijon mustard
1/4 egg yolk
1 tablespoon red wine vinegar
3/4 cup olive oil
Salt and pepper to taste

For the garnish:
4 ounces white asparagus, blanched
4 ounces French beans, blanched
4 tomato slices (cut in half)

For the beef, remove all fat from outside of strip loin. Rub 1 tablespoon salt and 1 tablespoon ground white pepper on each side of steak. Wrap tightly in plastic film and refrigerate for 2 days.

Remove plastic wrap and pound 1 tablespoon crushed peppercorns into each side of loin. Sear in smoking hot oil (approximately 15 seconds each side). Refrigerate until completely cool. Smoke sirloin steak, using hickory

chips, for approximately 2 hours, using "cold smoke method." Refrigerate until ready to use. (This will keep in refrigerat for several days.)

For the watercress sauce, finely chop watercress (leaves only) and chervil (stems removed) and put in stainless ste bowl with mustard, yolk and vinegar. Mix together with a wire whisk and let sit for minutes. Slowly add oil to watercress mi ture while mixing with the whip. Season with salt and pepper.

For assembly, place asparagus on top half of plate in a fan shape. Lay green beans on top of asparagus. Place 4-5 slices of smoked strip loin (sliced on the bias, very thin) on bottom half of plate, overlapping the slices. Put 2 tomato halves on each side of meat. Drizzle meat with watercress sauce. Serve cold.

TENDERLOIN OF BEEF WITH SHALLOT CONFIT

For the tenderloin:
1 pound Certified Angus Beef
   tenderloin
Salt and pepper to taste
1 tablespoon oil
1 tablespoon butter

For the potato and apple nest:
1 potato
1 apple
Salt and pepper to taste

For the shallot confit:
6 shallots
1 tablespoon sugar
Salt and pepper to taste
1 tablespoon butter

For the assembly:
1 cup uncooked spinach
1 tablespoon butter
Salt and pepper to taste

For the sauce:
1 shallot
1/2 cup white wine
1 cup veal demi-glace
1 tablespoon prepared mustard
Salt and pepper to taste
1 tablespoon butter

For the tenderloin, trim of all fat. Using string, tie tenderloin up at 1-inch intervals. Salt and pepper and sear in oil and butter. Roast in oven at 350 degrees F for 10 minutes. Set aside and let rest.

For the nest of potatoes and apples, finely grate one potato and one apple and mix together. Season with salt and pepper to taste. Place in two buttered four-inch Teflon-coated molds with one-inch sides. Cook over low heat until golden brown, then flip over and cook other side until golden brown.

For the shallot confit, place 6 shallots in a small roasting pan. Add sugar, salt, pepper and butter. Cover with aluminum foil and cook at 400 degrees F for 30 minutes.

For the sauce, finely chop one shallot, place in roasting pan used for tenderloin and deglaze with white wine. Let reduce by half and add demi-glace. Let reduce again and add mustard, salt and pepper to taste. Finish with butter and strain.

For assembly, sauté spinach with butter, salt and pepper until cooked. Place spinach flat in middle of plate and place nest of potatoes and apples on top. Place 3 confit of shallots in equal intervals around the outside of the nest of potatoes and apples. Slice beef into 6 equal medallions. Place 3 medallions of tenderloin between each confit of shallots. Spoon the sauce all around the plate.

ROAST TENDERLOIN WITH TOMATO AND CUCUMBER SALAD

(Serves 2)

Georges
Perrier

For the beef:
1 pound Certified Angus Beef
  tenderloin
Oil to cover
1/4 cup red wine vinegar
Bay leaf and thyme sprig

For the salad:
2 ripe tomatoes
1 cucumber
1/4 cup walnut oil
2 tablespoons sherry wine vinegar
1 tablespoon chopped parsley
1 tablespoon chopped chives
Salt and pepper to taste
1 peeled potato

For the sauce:
10 fresh morels
Madeira
1 cup veal demi-glace
1 teaspoon butter

For the beef, trim tenderloin of all
fat and place in a stainless steel pan
along with oil, red wine vinegar, bay leaf
and thyme sprig. Cover pan and marinate
for six hours in the refrigerator.

For the salad, peel and de-seed
tomatoes and slice cucumber very thin.
Marinate in walnut oil and sherry vinegar.
Add parsley and chives. Season with salt
and pepper. Slice gaufrette potatoes on
ribbed blade of the mandolin, turn 1/4 turn

to get the checkerboard effect. Deep fry
350 degree oil until golden brown. Plac
on a dry towel and season.

Remove beef from marinade and sea
in very hot oil. Place in oven to finish co
ing, about 12 minutes.

For the sauce, sauté morels in the
same pan used to sear tenderloin,
deglaze with Madeira, reduce by half, a
demi-glace and finish with butter. Adjus
seasoning.

For assembly, alternate tomato and
cucumber in center of the plate. Slice be
thinly across the grain and arrange on th
edges of the tomato and cucumber sala
Place gaufrette potatoes on the top sid
the salad. Pour sauce over bottom half o
the meat and serve.

ENRY
ALLER

rmer Chef
The White
ouse
otomac,
aryland

Henry Haller had a longer tenure at 1600 Pennsylvania Avenue than any of the presidents for whom he cooked. The White House chef prepared 250 state dinners and pot roast suppers for five of the nation's first families and their guests during his 21 years in the kitchen.

And now that Haller has retired, with time to spend skiing, visiting with his family, consulting, and promoting his book "The White House Family Cookbook" (Random House, $19.95), Haller is content that he held the highest chef's job in the land.

The native of Switzerland, who cooked in Bern, Switzerland, Montreal and New York City before coming to Washington, was a chef with a sense of survival. If the first lady wanted a salad prepared a certain way, Haller did it. If a president orchestrated an important dinner without much notice, Haller did his best to make the event a success. He has said while a White House chef may have his or her ideas as to how a meal should be served, you must do it the President's way.

Haller was hired to the White House kitchen in 1966 when newly inaugurated President Lyndon Johnson was looking for a top-quality chef. He recalls the FBI checking on his personal habits - whether he drank too much or stayed out late at night. Haller passed those tests and he followed the Kennedy's chef Rene Verdon to the White House. Prior to the Eisenhowers, Navy stewards were responsible for preparing the first family meals.

While part of his job has been to keep national secrets well secured, normally unflappable Haller divulges some interesting tidbits about White House life in his book. Ronald Reagan liked his beef cooked well-done. Gerald Ford preferred solid Midwestern food. Nancy Reagan took Polaroid snapshots of dishes so that the kitchen and wait staff would know how to prepare and serve them at her parties, he said.

SWISS STEAK WITH POLENTA

(erves 6)

For the beef:
3 tablespoons butter
3 medium-sized onions, thinly sliced
6 garlic cloves, minced
1 tablespoon salt
1 teaspoon freshly ground black pepper

1 tablespoon fresh thyme leaves, chopped or 1 teaspoon dried thyme
Flour
3 2-pound Certified Angus Beef top sirloin butt steaks, about 1 1/2-inch thick
2 tablespoons vegetable oil

2 bay leaves
3 cups beef stock, heated
12 ounces beer
3 cups julienne of carrot, leeks and celery (1 cup of each)
2 tablespoons chopped fresh parsley
1 bunch of parsley for decoration

continued on page 45

BOILED BEEF WITH HORSERADISH SAUCE

Henry Haller

(Serves 6)

For the beef and vegetables:
3 quarts water
6 pound piece Certified Angus Beef top sirloin butt
1 tablespoon salt
1 bay leaf
6 small onions
3 ribs celery, tops cut off, leaving the bottom 4 inches
2 bunches baby carrots
6 red skin potatoes

For the spice bag:
Cheesecloth
1 teaspoon dried thyme
1 teaspoon dried marjoram
24 peppercorns
4 whole cloves

For the horseradish sauce:
2 tablespoons butter
1 1/2 tablespoons all-purpose flour
1 1/2 cups beef stock
Salt
Pinch of freshly grated nutmeg
Pinch of white pepper
1 tablespoon Worcestershire sauce
1/2 cup fresh horseradish or 3 tablespoons of pressed horse- radish from a jar
2 tablespoons heavy cream

For the garnish:
Parsley sprigs
Paprika

For the beef and vegetables, using a 1/2 gallon-sized soup pot, combine wat meat, salt and bay leaf. Combine ingredients for the spice bag and add to Bring to a boil and skim off any foam. B meat slowly with the cover ajar, for 45 minutes. Add the onions and celery to t boiling beef. After about 30 minutes, remove the vegetables from the bouillon and keep warm. Add carrots and potato and cook until done. Remove them from bouillon and keep warm with the other vegetables and a small amount of bouil lon. Check the meat for tenderness. Wh the meat is cooked, turn off the heat under the soup pot and make the horse- radish sauce.

continued on page 45

HARTMUT HANDKE

e Greenbrier
hite Sulphur
rings, West
ginia

A commanding figure at over six feet tall, Hartmut Handke, executive chef of The Greenbrier in White Sulphur Springs, W. Va., is much respected for his presence and his cooking at this resort, which is tucked gracefully into the Allegheny range of the Appalachian mountains.

Whether he's greeting out-of-town visitors at the nearby airport or is juggling a five-pound weight in the resort's exercise room, the chef is always recognized by longtime Greenbrier guests. "Those weights keep you in shape to stir the sauces, don't they, Chef," a gray-haired admirer coos.

German-born Handke grins and agrees but doesn't let on that at sunrise each morning it's laps in the pool or a workout in the weight room that keeps his nearly 50-year-old physique trim. And while he says he "raised the average age of the Olympic team," it was his fellow 1988 U.S. Culinary team members who marveled at his energy.

Handke apprenticed at the Hotel Europaeischer Hof in Baden-Baden and worked in hotels in Switzerland, Canada and the Caribbean before coming to the Athletic Club of Columbus (Ohio) in 1977 as executive chef. Handke's first international culinary show was in 1980 at the Culinary Olympics in Frankfurt, and he worked out of a kitchen in his hometown of Schotten, about 15 miles north of Frankfurt. Handke competed in the 1984 and 1988 Olympics as a member of the U.S. Culinary Team.

Handke was seeking a challenge when he came to The Greenbrier in 1986. The sheer numbers excited him - the chance of doing $15 million in food and beverage a year (10 times what he was used to in Columbus) and using 12 tons of chocolate and $20,000 in fresh herbs annually.

Here Handke works with Rod Stoner, director of food and beverage, and has added finesse to a food service menu that has been built on traditions like serving de rigueur biscuits and corn bread at meals. Tradition is important to The Greenbrier, as many of the staff have been with the resort for 40 years.

In 1778 Amanda Anderson, a sufferer of rheumatism, leaped out of the sulphur waters here and said she had been cured. Thus The Greenbrier was born. It originally was a summer resort, but today it is open year round with the heaviest business from May through October.

Whereas the resort is suited to high tea and starched linen, the rustic environs outside The Greenbrier call for cold beer and hunting gear. Handke said he is faced with excusing chefs who are accustomed to taking days off during deer hunting season, and his wife Margot must shop for groceries over the state line in Virginia.

Beef Brisket with Spätzle

Recipe on page 45

BEEF TENDERLOIN TIPS "MEXICALI"

(Serves 8)

For the beef tenderloin:

1 1/2 pounds Certified Angus Beef
   tenderloin tips
1 jalapeño pepper, cut in julienne
   strips
1/4 cup pinot noir
1 1/2 cups beef or veal demi-glace
1/2 cup well cooked black beans
1/2 cup well cooked black-eyed peas
1/2 cup corn kernels

1/3 cup plum tomato concasse
1 tablespoon finely diced red onions
1/2 teaspoon parsley
1 tablespoon olive oil
1 teaspoon apple cider vinegar
Salt and pepper to taste
8 green onions
1 egg, beaten
1/2 avocado, cut in 8 wedges
1 cup ground almonds
8 flour tortillas, shaped into horns

For the beef, sauté beef tenderloin ti
and julienned jalapeño quickly in hot sk
let. When beef is medium-rare, remove
from skillet and reserve. Deglaze skille
with pinot noir, add demi-glace and sim
mer for a few minutes. Add meat to
sauce. Remove from heat and reserve.

Have black beans, black-eyed peas,
corn, concasse, onions and parsley
marinated with olive oil, vinegar, salt an
pepper. (Can be done in advance, but
should be warmed prior to serving).

Blanch green onions and season with
salt and pepper to taste. Egg wash
avocado wedges, bread with almond
crumbs and pan fry. Arrange flour tortill
in the shape of horns on plate. Place be
bean mixture, fried avocado and onions
with them.

CHARRED BEEF WITH SMOKED MARINATED BELL PEPPERS

(Serves 8)

For the beef:
1 pound Certified Angus Beef eye
 of round
1 red bell pepper
1 yellow bell pepper
1 green bell pepper
1 teaspoon olive oil
Salt and pepper
1 cup sour cream
1 tablespoon chives, cut

For the beef, season with salt and pepper and char beef in an iron skillet. Cool, wrap in plastic wrap and place in freezer. Peel peppers, poach and hot smoke quickly. Cut in julienne. Marinate with olive oil, salt and pepper. Mix sour cream with chives, salt and pepper. Reserve.

To serve, when beef is a little frozen, slice very thin. Arrange on plate, garnish with peppers and chive sour cream.

T-BONE STEAK FOR TWO

(Serves 2)

For the beef:
1 2-3 pound Certified Angus Beef
    T-bone steak from short loin
Salt and pepper

For the garnish:
2 cups mixed, cooked pinto, kidney,
    lima beans and black-eyed peas
1 cup prepared barbecue sauce
4 ears corn, grilled
Gaufrette   potatoes sliced from two
    large Idaho potatoes
8 pods okra, steamed

For the cornmeal mush:
1 cup water
1 cup milk
1 cup yellow cornmeal
Salt and pepper to taste

For the beef, season with salt and pepper and sear on a grill for 5 minutes each side. Finish cooking in a 350-degree F oven for 15 minutes. Let rest at least 10 minutes after cooking and keep warm.

For the garnish, combine bean mixture with barbecue sauce. Grill corn and deep-fry potatoes until crisp. Make slit in okra and remove seeds.

For the cornmeal mush, bring water and milk to a boil. Reduce heat and add corn meal. Let simmer 5 minutes and cook until thickened. Season with salt and pepper. Stuff okra pods with this mixture.

To serve, slice steak into two portions and arrange on platter with garnish of vegetables.

THOMAS CATHERALL

Cherokee Town & Country Club
Atlanta, Georgia

If Thomas Catherall had his way, the world wouldn't joke about English cooking. This native of Newcastle-upon-Tyne, England - a city located in the north-eastern corner of the country, close to the Scottish border - however, knows the last laugh isn't on him.

Catherall, who apprenticed at Newcastle's Royal Turks Head Hotel and has worked in kitchens in Bermuda and Barbados before coming to the United States, is one of the finest products any British kitchen has produced.

Presently, he is executive chef of the Cherokee Town & Country Club in Atlanta, which does $4 million in food and beverage business annually. At the private club Catherall oversees a staff of 40 cooks, and he serves a sophisticated membership receptive to his fresh, regional style of cooking.

"Sure, we offer fried chicken on the Sunday buffet," Catherall said. But more often you'll see grilled grouper with Caribbean seasoning, wok-charred tuna and velvety peach mousse in pecan lace baskets. Catherall, who said he serves "club food of the 90s," seeks out his specialty in-gredients like organically grown lettuces from a nearby farm and free-range veal from Virginia. Just a few of Catherall's kudos include becoming a Certified Master Chef at the Culinary Institute of America in 1985 and a gold-medal-win-ning member of the 1988 U.S. Culinary Team that competed in Frankfurt.

In order to participate on the olympic team, Catherall had to relinquish his British citizenship, which he did with some reservation. He has fond memories of England, one of which is his mother's roast lamb served on Sundays.

CARPACCIO OF BEEF JAPANESE STYLE

(Serves 4)

For the beef:
12 ounces Certified Angus Beef
   tenderloin, trimmed well
1 1/2 cups sliced shiitake mushrooms
4 tablespoons olive oil
1 teaspoon sesame oil
1 teaspoon soy sauce
1 teaspoon water
1 teaspoon prepared chili-garlic
   paste (see note)

For the garnish:
1/2 cup daikon sprouts
1 tablespoon toasted sesame seeds
Olive oil for brushing carpaccio

For the beef, wrap tenderloin in plastic wrap and place in freezer until almost frozen. Meanwhile, sauté mushrooms in olive oil. Combine sesame oil, soy sauce, water and chili-garlic paste in separate bowl. Add this mixture to sautéed mushrooms and set aside. Slice beef on a slicing machine very thin. Arrange slices on plates, leaving a space in the center for mushroom mixture.

To garnish, mix daikon sprouts with mushroom mixture. Spoon into center of plates. Arrange sesame seeds around border and brush beef with olive oil.

Note: Chili-garlic paste can be found at Oriental markets.

OUTH-OF-THE-BORDER FLANK STEAK

For the beef:
1 to 1 1/2 pounds Certified Angus
  Beef flank steak

For the marinade:
1 cup soy sauce
1 cup prepared barbecue sauce
1/2 cup Worcestershire sauce
2 tablespoons sesame oil
2 cups vegetable oil
2 bay leaves
Salt and pepper to taste
1 teaspoon minced garlic
1 tablespoon hot pepper sauce

For the garnish:
Flour tortillas
2 avocados, cut in half and fanned
Jalapeño peppers

For the Mexican relish:
1 green bell pepper, cored and
  seeded
1 red bell pepper, cored and seeded
1 medium tomato, peeled and seeded
1 jalapeño pepper, seeded
1 small onion
2 tablespoons prepared picante sauce

For the corn timbale:
2 tablespoons butter
1 ear fresh corn, shaved
1 tablespoon diced red pepper
1 teaspoon chopped green onion
1 egg
1 egg yolk
1 cup heavy cream
Salt and pepper to taste
Butter to grease molds

For the marinade, combine soy sauce, barbecue sauce, Worcestershire sauce, sesame oil, vegetable oil, bay leaves, salt, pepper, garlic and hot pepper sauce. Marinate beef for at least 48 hours.

For the relish, finely dice peppers, tomato and onion and add picante sauce.

For the beef, when ready to cook, grill flank steak over charcoal until medium-rare. Slice on the bias.

For the corn timbale, melt the butter in a skillet and sauté the corn, pepper and onion until soft. Cool, strain and set aside. In a mixing bowl, combine the egg, egg yolk and cream. Mix until well blended. Add the sautéed vegetables. Season to taste with salt and pepper. Butter 4 timbale molds and fill with the mixture. Place timbales in a water bath and bake in a preheated 350 degree oven for 20 minutes.

To serve, place flank steak on plate along with corn timbale. Place relish to the side, and garnish with flour tortillas, avocado and jalapeño pepper.

A CONTEMPORARY STEAK AND KIDNEY PIE

Thomas Catherall

(Serves 2)

For the filling:
4 tablespoons olive oil
8 ounces Certified Angus Beef top
  sirloin butt, cut into 1-inch cubes
2 lamb kidneys, trimmed of fat and
  diced
6 pearl onions, peeled
1 carrot, peeled and sliced into
  1-inch rounds
1/2 cup shiitake mushrooms
1/2 cup red wine
1 cup veal demi-glace
Salt and pepper to taste

For the pastry:
4 ounces puff pastry

For the filling, heat olive oil in a heavy-bottomed sauce pot. Sear beef cubes and kidney. Stir and cook for 3 minutes. Add onions, carrots and mushrooms. Cook 10 minutes more, then deglaze with red wine. Add demi-glace and salt and pepper to taste. Simmer for 30 minutes or until meat is tender. Remove from heat. Turn into an ovenproof dish and set aside to cool.

For the pastry, roll puff pastry 1/8-inch thick. Drape over the lid of an ovenproof dish or place directly over meat filling. Bake at 375 degrees until golden.

AUGUST SCHREINER

Augusto's Cuisine, Hotel Excelsior San Juan, Puerto Rico

Island ingredients have rubbed off on August Schreiner, chef of Augusto's Cuisine in the Hotel Excelsior in San Juan, Puerto Rico.

In 1979 he prepared a gourmet society dinner in San Juan, using just local produce and meats, proving that Puerto Rican food is of a style all its own. And in this 86-seat restaurant he opened a little over a year ago, Schreiner is free to experiment with island root vegetables, seafood and tropical produce.

"You can't beat locally produced food for freshness," he said. "But the island beef is not very good." For that reason Schreiner tasted and selected Certified Angus Beef to serve at his restaurant and in the restaurants of the Caribe Hilton where he was executive chef prior to Augusto's.

Born in Austria, Schreiner began cooking in 1966, and he did his apprenticeship in Salzburg at the Cafe Glockenspiel and Schloss Hellbrunn before transferring to the Grand Hotel in Paris in 1969.

He joined the Hilton hotel company in 1971 at the Dusseldorf Hilton and later traveled to Bogota, Colombia, Condado Beach, Puerto Rico and the Caribe Hilton in San Juan. He was recognized by Hilton in 1982, 1983 and 1984 with the Maurice Raymond Award as being an outstanding executive chef.

When Schreiner leaves the island, it's usually to compete in culinary shows. In 1984 he was captain of the first national team from the Caribbean to attend the Culinary Olympics in Frankfurt.

PAUPIETTES OF BEEF

(Serves 1)

For the beef:
2 4-ounce Certified Angus Beef
   top round (inside) slices
Salt and pepper to taste
1 garlic clove, smashed
2 slices fat back
1 peeled carrot
1 peeled parsnip root

For the garnish:
3 pods okra, blanched
2 sweet peppers, blanched
Pinch minced jalapeño peppers
1 tablespoon vegetable oil
1 teaspoon browned butter
Grated carrot, fresh herbs

For the dish:
Vegetable oil, 1 cup red wine
1 1/2 cups brown veal stock

For the beef, flatten meat with a meat mallet, season with salt and pepper and rub with garlic. Place fat back slice on top of meat, carrot and parsnip on each meat slice and roll. Secure tightly with butcher string.

Sear beef in hot oil in a frying pan. Deglaze with wine, add veal stock and braise, covered, over low heat for about 35 to 40 minutes. Remove meat, strain the sauce and keep warm.

For the garnish, sauté okra and peppers in a mixture of oil and browned butter. Cut the tips off paupiettes to expose the filling and place on plate with garnish of peppers and okra. Top beef with carrot, garnish with herbs and surround with sauce from the pan.

PAPAYA MARINATED TOP BUTT STEAK

(Serves 1)

For the marinade:
2 tablespoons olive oil
Juice of 1/2 lime
2 teaspoons papaya puree
1 small garlic clove, crushed
6 cilantro leaves
Salt and pepper to taste

For the steak:
1 8-ounce Certified Angus Beef top
   sirloin butt steak
Salt and pepper

For the garnish:
1/2 pear, blanched and filled with
   ratatouille
papaya balls
Cilantro, baby squash and peppers

For the marinade, combine all ingredients.

For the beef, marinate the meat for 3 hours. Pat dry with paper towels. Season with salt and pepper and broil to desired doneness. Garnish with pear half filled with ratatouille, papaya balls, cilantro, baby squash and peppers.

(serves 2)

For the curry sauce:
1 cup chopped apple
1 cup chopped eggplant
1 cup chopped banana
Vegetable oil
1 teaspoon caraway seed
1 teaspoon coriander seed
1 teaspoon tumeric
2 tablespoons shallots
2 garlic cloves
1 teaspoon lemon grass
1 teaspoon coriander root
1 teaspoon fresh ginger
1 chile pepper
1 cup chicken stock
1/2 cup unsweetened coconut milk
Salt and pepper to taste

For the pineapple cups:
1 pineapple
1 tablespoon honey
1 teaspoon grated fresh ginger
2 tablespoons fresh lime juice

For the beef:
1 pound Certified Angus Beef
   tenderloin tips
1 teaspoon oil
4 tablespoons rum
Salt and pepper

For the garnish:
Rice timbales, zucchini, red bell pepper, hot peppers, pineapple chunks and green onion frills

For the curry sauce, sauté apple, eggplant and banana in vegetable oil. Roast caraway seeds, coriander and tumeric. Crush shallots, garlic, lemon grass, coriander root, ginger and chile in mortar. Add all three mixtures to chicken stock and cook for 10 minutes. Add coconut milk and cook for 10 more minutes, then puree and strain. Season with salt and pepper and set aside.

For the pineapple cups, cut two pineapple rings approximately 1 1/2-inch thick. Remove peel, and trim to 3 1/2 inches in diameter. Scoop out center to form a cup. Combine honey, ginger and lime juice and baste pineapple cups with this mixture. Glaze under broiler.

For the beef, season with salt and pepper and sauté beef tenderloin tips in hot oil. Deglaze with rum, add the curry sauce and cook for 1 minute. Place the coated beef tips in the pineapple cups and garnish.

RALPH DiORIO

Ralph DiOrio and his wife Denise Fugo took a gamble that Cleveland's struggling economy would improve in the early 1980s.

The husband and wife team, natives of the Cleveland suburbs and high school sweethearts, were working in sales and as a stock broker, respectively, when they decided to switch gears and place their $40,000 profit from renovating a home in Chicago into opening a restaurant in a development called the Flats along Cleveland's Cuyahoga River.

That foresight has paid off, for Cleveland is, indeed, enjoying a financial resurgence. And their restaurant called Sammy's has been open less than 10 years and will do $4.5 million in food and beverage sales this year.

DiOrio handles the back, with a team of five cooks, and his wife is at the front. "We're a strong team," Ms. Fugo said. "Ever since we were in high school and I planned the school proms and he built the props for them, we've been working together well."

Sammy is neither Ralph's name, his father's or anyone special. Just a "masculine, catchy" name that DiOrio and his wife thought people would remember. And they have, especially the male business patrons who account for 40 percent of the restaurant's business.

Sammy's is located on the second floor of a warehouse, renovated by family and friends, Ms. Fugo said. Its interior of exposed red brick and rough timber is softened by mauve paint and fresh white muslin curtains outlining wrap-around

glass windows that offer you a view of Cuyahoga or "crooked" river.

The food is best described as being "contemporary American," Ms. Fugo sa "Classic techniques and creative ingredients." While neither she nor her h band have any formal culinary training they both came from half Italian, half Slavic families "whose largest room in house was always the kitchen," she sa

Italian sausage was made fresh, the relatives were in the produce business, and after graduating from college, they began to cook and entertain frequently. Sammy's was originally opened as a ra bar, then gravitated towards serving sandwiches, soups and small meals. Fo years after its opening DiOrio said he w the best qualified to cook, and there he has stayed. In addition to supervising th restaurant cooking staff, he coordinates large catering functions.

"It has taken us some years to learn business," said Ms. Fugo, "but we have learned it from the bottom up."

TOP SIRLOIN STIR FRY ON CELLOPHANE NOODLES

Recipe on page 45

ENDERLOIN TIPS WITH THAI STYLE BARBECUE SAUCE

(erves 4)

For the barbecue sauce:
3 tablespoons hoisin sauce
1 tablespoon honey
1 1/2 teaspoons rice vinegar
1 tablespoon soy sauce
1/2 cup tomato puree
1 green onion, minced
1/2 orange, juiced, 1 clove garlic
1 tablespoon Thai hot paste
Salt and white pepper to taste

For the saffron rice:
1 teaspoon clarified butter
5 1/2 ounces basmati rice
1 cup chicken stock
1/2 teaspoon saffron
Pinch cayenne pepper
2 tablespoons diced white onion
3/4 green onion, sliced
2 tablespoons diced red bell pepper
Salt and white pepper

For the beef:
1 1/2 pounds Certified Angus Beef
 tenderloin tips, cubed
Salt and pepper
Vegetable oil
1 red pepper, seeded and cubed
1 golden pepper, seeded and cubed
12 cherry tomatoes
12 shiitake mushrooms

For the sauce, combine all ingredients and mix well. Season to taste with salt and white pepper. Set aside.

For the saffron rice, brush pan with clarified butter. Add rice, chicken stock, saffron, cayenne pepper and onion. Stir. Cover pan and bake at 400 degrees F for 1 hour and 10 minutes. When rice is done remove foil and stir in green onions and red pepper. Season to taste with salt and white pepper. For the beef, place meat and vegetables alternately on skewer, season with salt and pepper and brush with oil. Grill on both sides to medium-rare. Remove from grill and brush generously with barbecue sauce. Place on saffron rice and garnish with more sauce.

CERTIFIED ANGUS BEEF

LUCIEN VENDOME

Corporate
Executive
Chef, Stouffer
Hotels&Resorts
Solon, Ohio

**Chef Nicola Torres and Chef
Lucien Vendome (seated)**

Lucien Vendome was a contented, successful executive chef who chose to give up the everyday toil in the kitchen for the life of corporate chef. And in so doing, this corporate chef of Stouffer Hotels & Resorts has had to wear two hats.

Five days a month he must don his toque and move into Stouffer kitchens nationwide as he strategically plans new openings and carefully works out kinks. The remainder of the time the 38-year-old French chef wears the hat of a businessman - attending meetings, traveling across the country, and dining in new restaurants.

Born in a town in the French Alps called Aix-les-Bains, Vendome left his Savoie home to attend cooking school in Paris and to afterwards apprentice on the luxury liner the S.S. France. He made his first U.S. stop in Philadelphia, where he worked at the restaurant Latrousse from 1974 to 1976. And then he joined the

Omni International Hotel group as chef [of] the French Restaurant in the Atlanta O[mni] from 1976 to 1978.

Here Vendome and "my whole briga[de] from the bankrupt S.S. France" gained [na]tional attention. He was soon snatched [up] by Stouffer's, where he has worked as [cor]porate chef for the last 11 years.

Vendome has opened 20 hotels and their restaurants in his tenure, such as [St.] Nicholas in the Mayflower in Washingto[n,] the French Connection in Cleveland, Ra[f]fles in Maui, and Cinnabar in Atlanta. Hi[s] next project is a Mediterranean restaura[nt] in the Stouffer's hotel in Palm Springs, California.

"I adore traveling, really," said Vendome, who said dining in new restauran[ts] is his way of "comparative shopping."

"If I get a great idea from San Francis[c]co, I try to use that idea in Cleveland. It'[s] very enjoyable," he added.

PAUPIETTES OF BEEF "SHINUAH"

(Serves 2)

For the paupiettes:
6 ounces Certified Angus Beef top
   sirloin butt
6 medium shrimp
4 tablespoons roasted pine nuts
Salt and pepper to taste
1 egg white
4 tablespoons cornstarch
1 teaspoon sesame oil
Leek slices
Fresh cilantro, fresh chives
Plum noodles

For the sauce mixture:
1 diced red chile pepper
1 teaspoon minced green onion
1 clove garlic, minced
1/2 cup chicken stock
1/2 tablespoon red wine vinegar
1/2 tablespoon soy sauce
1/2 tablespoon brown sugar
1 teaspoon tapioca powder
1 tablespoon dry sherry
1 teaspoon sesame oil

For the sauce, stir the red chile and green onion in hot oil. Add the remaining sauce ingredients except sesame oil. Stir and reduce over medium heat. Add sesame oil.

For the paupiettes of beef, cut the sirl[oin] across the grain into 6 - 8 square slices [ap]proximately 3/16-inch thick. Devein the shrimp, split along the back lengthwise i[n] half. Chop pine nuts finely to a paste. To assemble the paupiettes, lay 1 piece of beef on cutting board, sprinkle with salt a[nd] pepper. Place 1/2 a shrimp in the center. Spread 1/4-inch of pine nut paste and top with the other half of shrimp. Roll the bee[f] and seal with egg white and chill. Dip eac[h] paupiette in egg white first. Then cornstarch to coat evenly. Sizzle and brown the paupiettes in hot oil and remov[e.] Remove excess oil from wok and add sauce mixture. Bring to boil. Add beef rol[ls.] Reduce sauce enough to cover the paupi[et]tes. Drizzle with sesame oil.

Garnish with leeks, chives, cilantro and plum noodles.

NOTE: The two halves of shrimp shoul[d] be placed with the tail atop the long end i[n] order to produce a uniform paupiette.

OBSTER AND BEEF CARPACCIO

(rves 8)

For the garnish:
Arugula
Yellow tomato slices
Sautéed sliced shiitake mushrooms
Vinaigrette made with extra virgin
  olive oil
Olive oil
Chives, chopped
Fresh pepper to taste
Parmesan cheese
Brioche toast

For the carpaccio:
2 4-ounce lobster tails
Court bouillon
Spinach leaves
Aspic
2 pounds Certified Angus Beef top
  sirloin butt

For the carpaccio, poach the lobster tails in court bouillon. Chill and remove meat from carcass. Blanch the spinach leaves lightly. Wrap the lobster in spinach and coat with aspic. Shape the sirloin in a long round cylinder. Trim the fat. Hollow out the center. Fill the center with the lobster meat. Wrap in aluminum foil and shape into a round cylinder. Chill in the freezer for 45 - 60 minutes. Thinly slice the beef and place on the plate.

Garnish the plate with tossed arugula, tomato slices and shiitake slices in vinaigrette. Top the carpaccio with the olive oil, chopped chives and fresh pepper. Serve with grilled Parmesan brioche made by sprinkling Parmesan cheese on buttered brioche and running under the broiler.

SIRLOIN "SALADE BOURGOISE"

(Serves 4)

Lucien
Vendome

For the beef and marinade:
1/4 cup olive oil
3 onions, sliced
2 cloves garlic, minced
3 tablespoons cracked black
    peppercorns
1/2 tablespoon grated lemon peel
1 bunch cilantro, chopped
1 pound Certifed Angus Beef top
    sirloin butt

For the chick peas:
1 pound dried chick peas
1 quart chicken stock, and more
    as needed
1 onion, studded with cloves
1 clove garlic, chopped
1 carrot, chopped
1 rib celery, chopped
Pinch saffron

For the vinaigrette:
2 tablespoons extra virgin olive oil
2 tablespoons balsamic vinegar

For the goat cheese cigars:
4 ounces goat cheese
2 sprigs fresh basil
1 tablespoon toasted walnuts,
    chopped
3 tablespoons extra virgin olive oil
8 sheets phyllo dough
Egg white
Butter for sautéing

For the salad garnish:
Assorted seasonal greens
Extra virgin olive oil
Salt and pepper to taste

For the beef marinade, mix all ingredients and marinate beef for at least
24 hours.

For the chick peas, soak peas overnight
in cold water to cover.

The next day, drain sirloin of marinade
and trim. Grill until medium-rare or still
pink. Let rest.

To finish chick peas, drain of soaking
water and place in sauce pot with chicken

stock, onion, garlic, carrot and celery.
Bring to a boil, reduce heat and simme
until stock has reduced by half and the
add more as needed. Continue simmer
peas and adding stock until peas are ju
tender. In the last hour of cooking, add
fron to pan. When peas are tender,
remove from heat, drain, remove onion
garlic, carrot and celery and cool slight

For vinaigrette, combine oil and vineg
and pour over chick peas while still war

For the cigars, combine goat cheese
with chopped fresh basil, walnuts and c
Let marinate slightly. Drain cheese, res
ing the marinade and roll cheese in phy
dough in the shape of thin cigars. Each
sheet of phyllo should make 4 cigars. Y
will have more cigars than you need. Se
flaps with egg white. Brown cigars in bu
ter in a hot fry pan. Set aside.

For the salad, toss greens with
reserved cheese marinade and add mo
oil, salt and pepper if needed.

To serve, place greens on plate with
slices of beef. Decorate with goat chees
cigars and a garnish of chick peas.

~ISS STEAK WITH POLENTA

~nry Haller

~n page 27

For the polenta:
1 quart beef bouillon or stock
1/4 teaspoon freshly ground white
  pepper
1 tablespoon butter
1 cup yellow cornmeal
1 tablespoon vegetable oil
4 tablespoons Parmesan cheese
2 tablespoons butter, melted

For the beef, melt butter in large sauté pan. Add onions and garlic and sauté until golden brown. Set aside. Season steaks with salt, pepper, fresh thyme and lightly sprinkle with flour. Heat oil in an iron skillet until very hot. Add the steaks and sear quickly on both sides.

Transfer steaks to the large sauté pan on top of the sautéed onions. Add bay leaves. Pour 2 cups of the heated beef stock and the 12 ounces of beer over the meat. Cover and simmer slowly for one hour. Cook the julienne of vegetables in the remaining cup of heated beef stock for 15 minutes. Keep warm in the bouillon. Turn steaks over and simmer for 20 minutes more. When the steaks are tender, keep them warm in the sauce.

For the polenta, in a 2-quart saucepan, mix bouillon with pepper and 1 tablespoon butter, bringing to a boil. Add cornmeal, stirring with a wire whisk. Cook over low heat for 10 minutes or until thick. Cover

and simmer over very low heat for 20 minutes, stirring often with plastic or wooden spoon. Brush a baking sheet with oil and spread out the polenta evenly about 1/2-inch thick. Sprinkle with the Parmesan cheese and dribble the melted butter on top of the cheese. Let cool slightly. Then chill in refrigerator for at least one hour or until firm to the touch. Using a round cookie cutter, make 18 two-inch rounds. Bake polenta rounds in 375 degree F oven on an upper shelf until golden brown.

To serve the steaks, arrange polenta rounds, cut in half, along one side of plate. Cut each steak at an angle into slices and arrange 8 slices along the other side of the plate. Cover steak with some of the sauce. (Serve the rest of the sauce separately.) Garnish steaks with vegetable juliennes. Sprinkle with parsley. Decorate the plate with some whole parsley and serve.

~ILED BEEF WITH HORSERADISH SAUCE

~nry Haller

~n page 28

For the sauce, in a small saucepan, heat butter, add flour and mix with a wire whisk. Add beef stock and stir until sauce is smooth. Add salt if needed, nutmeg, white pepper and simmer for 10 minutes. Add Worcestershire, horseradish and cream. Stir. Keep warm.

Cut tops off onions, scoop out centers, and fill with the horseradish sauce, reserving the tops. Slice the potatoes. Arrange heated vegetables

attractively on a large dinner plate.

Cut meat across the grain in 1/8-inch thick slices. Arrange along the vegetables. Pour a little hot bouillon over the meat and vegetables. Place onion with the horseradish sauce to the side of plate, and place top of onion alongside.

Garnish plate with whole parsley sprigs and sprinkle horseradish sauce with paprika. Serve very hot. Serve horseradish sauce separately.

~EF BRISKET WITH SPÄTZLE

~rtmut
~ndke

~n page 29

~rves 4)

For the spätzle:
2 eggs
1 1/2 cups all-purpose flour
1/2 cup water
Salt and pepper to taste
1/4 teaspoon baking powder

For the brisket:
2 quarts beef broth
1/2 pound raw potatoes, diced in
  1/4-inch cubes
2 tablespoons leeks, cut on
  the diagonal
1 1/2 pounds Certified Angus Beef
  brisket, boiled and cut in
  1/2-inch cubes
1/2 pound spätzle
1/2 cup diced onions
2 tablespoons butter
2 tablespoons short cut chives

For the spätzle, beat eggs and combine with flour, water, salt, pepper and baking powder. Set batter aside.

Bring beef broth to a boil with potatoes and leeks. When potatoes are done, add beef cubes. Pour spätzle batter through a colander or a spätzle cutter over stock. Cook until spätzle is done.

Caramelize diced onion in butter until golden brown and add to stew. Add chives. Serve in soup bowls.

~P SIRLOIN STIR FRY ON CELLOPHANE NOODLES

~lph DiOrio

~n page 40

~rves 4)

For the stir-fry sauce:
3 tablespoons fish sauce
1 1/2 tablespoons sweet and
  hot mustard
1/2 cup soy sauce, Juice of 1/2 lime
1/3 cup sake
Salt and white pepper to taste

For the beef:
1 1/2 pounds Certified Angus Beef
  top sirloin butt
Salt and pepper for seasoning
Oil for frying
20 snow peas
4 tablespoons red pepper slivers
1 cup prepared stir-fry sauce
Bean thread noodles

For the garnish:
Enoki mushrooms
Cilantro leaves

For the sauce, combine all ingredients and mix well. Season to taste with salt and white pepper. Set aside.

For the beef, cut meat into strips and season with salt and pepper. Heat oil in wok and add meat. Braise both sides of beef. Add snow peas, peppers and 1 cup of sauce. Simmer 2 minutes.

To serve, heat noodles and place on plate. Attractively arrange meat and noodles and garnish with enoki mushrooms and cilantro leaves.

PETER LOREN II

Opus One Detroit, Michigan

Roulade of Sirloin with Red Skin Potato Salad Recipe on page 66

Detroit native Peter Loren II feels fortunate to be in the kitchen at a time when Midwesterners are receptive to new, fresh cooking.

"Detroit has always been a town that appreciates high quality meat," said Loren, "but with upwardly mobile young people living here now, there is more room to experiment and more available money than there has been in Detroit for a long time."

Loren, chef of Opus One, a fine dining restaurant in downtown Detroit serving "progressive cosmopolitan cuisine," said while talent has been present in Midwestern kitchens, the patrons have been "too conservative." But "now we're feeling a different pulse," he said.

Loren grew up in the Detroit suburban area, graduated from the Culinary Institute of America in 1974 and taught at the CIA for a year afterward. "At that time it was quite prestigious to be selected to instruct. I taught everything from meat cutting to how to give cooking demonstrations."

Loren traveled back to Detroit and worked at several restaurants in the area, including the London Chop House and the Money Tree. Then, for eight years he was director and teacher at Monroe County Community College, and that allowed summers off to consult with the Sheraton Hotel Corporation. He opened the kitchen at Opus One about three years ago.

At 146-seat Opus One, Loren combines classical cooking with contemporary American cuisine. As much as possible made in-house, even the luncheon sandwich breads. "We make our own pastries, smoke all our meats, make our own vinegars and mayonnaises," Loren said.

He tries to use local, indigenous Michigan ingredients. "But if I have to go to California for the best quality at that moment, I will," the chef said.

Loren began using Certified Angus Beef when he opened Opus One. He tasted beef from various purveyors, but the Certified Angus Beef product won out. "Its taste was impressive," he said, "and I felt it was a marketable and consistent product."

ROASTED AND STUFFED TOP SIRLOIN

(serves 4)

For the stuffing:
3 cups shiitake mushrooms, cut
 into julienne strips
2 tablespoons minced shallots
Clarified butter
Salt and pepper to taste
4 red bell peppers, roasted, peeled,
 and cut into julienne strips
2 cups fresh basil leaves, shredded
3 egg whites

For the beef:
2 14-ounce Certified Angus Beef top
 sirloin butt cap muscles
Vegetable oil

For the sauce:
1 small onion, diced
1 1/2 tablespoons clarified butter
1 1/2 tablespoons flour
1 1/4 cups hot milk
Salt and pepper to taste
1/2 pinch ground cloves
1/2 pinch nutmeg

For the garnish:
Chopped chives
Red skinned potatoes, cut into
 mushrooms, roasted and seasoned

For the stuffing, sauté mushrooms and shallots in clarified butter, season and chill. Combine this with peppers, basil and egg whites.

For the beef, cut a pocket in cap muscles. Stuff beef with stuffing mixture. Seal with a toothpick. Sear in hot oil and roast at 375 degrees F until medium-rare, about 30 minutes. Stuffing should be about 145 degrees F. Set aside.

For the sauce, saute onions in clarified butter until tender. Add flour to make roux. Cook 5 minutes on low heat. Add hot milk. Stir until smooth. Season to taste with the spices. Puree and strain through fine chinois.

To serve, slice beef and place on plate with sauce. Garnish sauce with chives. Garnish plate with potato mushrooms.

OPUS ONE
DETROIT

HICKORY SMOKED ROULADE OF STRIP LOIN BRO

(Serves 4)

For the sauce:
1/2 cup sour cream
1 teaspoon fresh oregano
1 teaspoon fresh thyme
1 teaspoon fresh basil
1 teaspoon fresh parsley
1 teaspoon minced garlic
1 tablespoon minced onion

For the garnish:
1 tablespoon chopped fresh Italian
herbs (oregano, basil, etc.)
1 tablespoon pink peppercorns

For the marinade:
Salt and pepper to taste
Vegetable oil to cover

For the beef:
2 14-ounce Certified Angus Beef
strip loin steaks
Hickory chips and charcoal
36 spears fresh asparagus, blanched
and cut into 4-inch lengths
8 puff pastry sticks, about 3/8- by
6-inches
Salt and pepper to taste
2/3 cup asparagus stems, cut
1/4-inch on the bias, blanched
2/3 cup red onion, cut into 1/4-inch
cubes
2/3 cup peeled, seeded and cubed
tomato

For the beef, marinate in salt, peppe
and oil overnight.

Cold smoke beef with hickory wood
chips and charcoal for 2 hours. Grill to
medium-rare. Chill. Slice on bias into
strips 4 to 5 inches long. Place asparag
(3 pieces per strip) in center of strip an
roll up. Place beef rolls atop two puff
pastry sticks and season with salt and p
per as needed.

Mix together minced asparagus stem
red onion and tomato.

Combine sauce ingredients in a
blender. Place pool of sauce on either
side of puff sticks and sprinkle asparag
mixture on top of sauce.

To serve, garnish with fresh herbs ar
pink peppercorns.

TUFFED BEEF MEDALLIONS WITH BASIL

rves 4)

For the beef:
12 roasted garlic cloves
12 fresh, blanched basil leaves
1 pound, 8 ounces Certified Angus
  Beef ground chuck
4 tablespoons cracked black
  peppercorns

For the garlic garnish:
4 garlic bulbs, tops cut off
4 tablespoons olive oil

For the sauce and garnish:
1/2 cup veal demi-glace
12 strips bacon, cut 1/2 by 4 inches,
  fried crisp and bundled
4 green onion strips, blanched
12 baby carrots, peeled, steamed
  and seasoned

For the beef, chill roasted garlic cloves. Wrap each with blanched basil leaves and stuff into interior of tear drop-fashioned 2-ounce patty of ground chuck. Coat one side with coarsely cracked black peppercorns. Broil or grill to proper doneness.

For the garlic garnish, drizzle bulbs with olive oil and roast at 350 degrees F until done, about 1 hour.

To sauce and garnish, heat veal demi-glace and spoon onto plate. Top with beef. Garnish with bacon strips that have been tied with green onions. Add carrots and garlic bulbs.

JEAN BANCHET
Former Owner/Chef Le Français
Culinary Consultant
Wheeling, Illinois

In 16 years, he has shown 50 chefs how to correctly make a Bearnaise, how to assemble soufflés without flour, and how to prepare satiny caramel sauce for dessert.

So it's not surprising that Jean Banchet's protégés crank out his recipes in their restaurants coast to coast. "It makes me feel good when the recipes work," said Banchet, "but not when they change the recipe. That makes me very upset."

continued on next page

enerous and enterprising, Banchet, ex-chef/proprietor of the famed Le ançais restaurant in Wheeling, Ill., is of the country's best culinary hers. Wise from experience and fresh change, Banchet's food appealed to t everyone who dined at this noble tion of fine dining, an hour's drive from ntown Chicago. Banchet still owns the ding, but the new proprietor/chef is and Liccioni.

his wild, curly chestnut mane and mis-evous eyes give Banchet the look of ashbuckler, not chef. The Frenchman long planned to turn the restaurant r to someone younger and move on to time consulting and collecting antique s. On occasion, you might have seen a rrari in Banchet's parking lot, but most his cars are kept in storage.

Devoting his time to consulting these days, the chef travels to Dallas, Newport Beach, Calif., and China consulting for hotels. He, like Paul Bocuse, has endorsed his share of products - knives, ice cream makers and miniature food processors.

Banchet said he cannot drop out of the culinary business because the "state of French cooking is not too hot in the United States right now." We've headed away from nouvelle cuisine, which he is glad of, recalling the worst meal of his life - fish with raspberry coulis. "But we're bound to return to traditional French cooking," he added.

The bistro food currently being prepared in the United States isn't authentic, Banchet said. "It's more Californian in style." He would like to create a true French bistro offering regional cooking and is contemplating opening one in Philadelphia with colleague Georges Perrier.

SAUTÉED FILET WITH CHASSEUR SAUCE

(Serves 2)

For the beef:
2 9-ounce Certified Angus Beef
 tournedos
1/2 cup clarified butter
Salt and pepper

For the sauce:
1 teaspoon chopped shallots
1 cup fresh, peeled and diced
 tomatoes
1 cup sliced mushrooms
1/2 cup white wine
1 cup veal demi-glace
1 teaspoon fresh tarragon
1/2 cup butter
Salt and pepper to taste

continued on page 66

CÔTE DE BOEUF WITH BLACK OLIVE SAUCE

(Serves 2)

Jean Banchet

For the beef:
2 12-ounce Certified Angus Beef
  rib eye steaks
1/2 cup clarified butter
1 tablespoon fresh butter
1 tablespoon minced shallots
1 teaspoon minced garlic
1/2 cup white wine
1 cup veal demi-glace
1/2 cup puree of black olives
1 cup unsalted butter
Salt and pepper to taste

For the garnish:
Cooked and seasoned baby
  vegetables
Fresh herbs
Sliced mushrooms

For the beef, season with salt and pepper, and sauté the 2 rib eye steaks with clarified butter and cook until medium-rare. Keep warm.

For the sauce, remove fat from the p[...] Add one tablespoon of fresh butter, sha[...] lots and garlic and cook for one minute[...] Add the white wine and reduce all the w[...] to syrup. Add demi-glace and reduce b[...] half. Add the puree of black olives and [...] for 1 minute. Remove from the heat an[...] add 1 cup of fresh butter, piece by piec[...] Do not boil the sauce again. Season to [...] taste and pour the sauce over the steak[...]

For the garnish, place vegetables, [...] herbs and mushrooms around plates.

ARK MILLER

yote Cafe
nta Fe, New Mexico

o dine with Mark Miller is to receive a les-
in anthropology. The Boston native
nt his early years studying more of the
ory and culture of foreign lands than of
r food.

But Miller has become a pioneer of new
uthwestern cooking, and at his Coyote
e restaurant in Santa Fe you not only
nple the tastes of Southwestern food,
u ingest some of the region's history.

When the student of Chinese art history
d anthropology moved to Berkeley,
lif., in 1967 to attend the University of
lifornia campus there - and later to teach -
introduced himself to a fresh, progressive
inary community. Berkeley was where
ce Waters opened the country French
ez Panisse restaurant where Miller and
her culinary figures such as
remiah Tower worked.

Miller later dabbled in eth-
flavors at the Fourth
eet Grill restaurant
Berkeley, and
ore specifically
outhwestern
stes at the
anta Fe Bar
d Grill,
so in
erkeley.

Miller's interest in anthropology and history gravitated
his palate toward this Southwestern style of cooking
as he felt it was America's oldest cuisine and one
worthy of study.

At the Fourth Street Grill he cooked over mesquite
coals. But when he moved to Santa Fe and opened
Coyote Cafe in 1987, he found another wood that
was even more indigenous to the area - pecan. No.
Pecan is not only grown in the Deep South; it is also
found in great abundance in Las Cruces, New
Mexico across the border from El Paso, Texas.

Since Miller has been in Santa Fe, which is called
the oldest city in the United States, his plates have become vibrant canvases of desert hues - yellow and
red peppers, green cacti and chestnut brown rich
sauces.

The Coyote Cafe seats 110 and is open for lunch
and dinner serving food that is influenced by Mexican
Hispanic and American regional styles. Yet, Miller is
quick to substitute a European technique or a different ingredient, just to keep the diners on their toes.

Menus change daily, but one of the most popular
Coyote Cafe dishes is the Cowboy Steak, Miller's
trademark. It calls for Certified Angus Beef and was
photographed for an early 1989 front of Bon Appetit
magazine. Miller uses the center cut filet, Porterhouse
and T-bone of Certified Angus Beef at
Coyote Cafe. Miller's dishes are
documented in his new cookbook called "Coyote Cafe:
Foods from the South-
west," by Mark Miller
and edited by John
Harrison (Ten-
Speed Press).

COWBOY STEAK WITH RED CHILI ONION RINGS

(Serves 4)

For the salsa:
2 small red onions, diced
2 pounds tomatoes, cut into
  1/4-inch pieces
6 tablespoons fresh lime juice
6 tablespoons finely chopped
  fresh cilantro
2 tablespoons finely chopped, seeded
  jalapeño chile peppers
2 tablespoons olive oil
Salt to taste

For the beef:
4 room-temperature 1 1/2 inch thick
  Certified Angus Beef rib steaks
  (T-bone or porterhouse steaks may
  also be used)
Salt and freshly ground pepper

For the onion rings:
4 white onions, cut into 1/16- to 1/8-
  inch wide rings
3 cups milk
3 cups sifted all-purpose flour
1/2 cup chili powder
2 tablespoons plus 2 teaspoons
  cornstarch
3 teaspoons salt
3 teaspoons ground cumin
2 teaspoons sugar
2 teaspoons Hungarian hot paprika
Vegetable oil (for frying)

For the salsa, soak red onion in water in large bowl for 1 hour. Drain thoroughly. Transfer to medium bowl. Add tomatoes, lime juice, cilantro, chile peppers, oil and salt, and toss well. Cover salsa with plastic wrap and refrigerate until ready to serve. (Can be prepared 6 hours ahead). Prepare barbecue over medium-high heat. Season steaks with salt and pepper, and grill to desired doneness (about 7 minutes per side for medium-rare). Transfer to plates. Drain salsa and spoon onto steaks. Serve steaks immediately with onion rings.

For the onion rings, soak onions in milk in large bowl for 1 hour. Drain thoroughly. Mix all remaining ingredients except oil in another large bowl. Dredge onions in flour mixture; shake off excess. Heat oil in large heavy saucepan to 375 degrees. Add onions in batches and cook until golden brown, about 45 seconds. Transfer to paper towels using slotted spoon; drain well. Serve immediately.

BEEF FILET WITH TOMATILLO CHIPOTLE SAUCE

(Serves 4)

For the sauce:
26 large tomatillos (about 2 pounds)
3 cloves garlic (unpeeled)
1 medium white onion, finely chopped
3 tablespoons olive oil
4 pieces of canned chipotle chiles in
  adobo sauce
2 teaspoons adobo sauce
1 bunch cilantro, leaves only
  (about 1 packed cup)
1 teaspoon salt
Juice of 1 lime

For the beef:
4 6-ounce Certified Angus Beef
  center-cut filets
Salt and pepper to taste
3 tablespoons olive oil
4 corn tortillas
3 tablespoons corn oil
4 slices fontina cheese, about
  1-ounce each

For the garnish:
Chopped cilantro

For the sauce, husk and wash the tomatillos under hot water. In a black iron skillet cook the tomatillos for 20 to 25 minutes over medium high heat until soft and blackened all over. Do not allow to dry out. Shake pan every couple of minutes. Roast the garlic until soft but not burnt (about 20 to 25 minutes), peel, and remove blackened parts. Sauté onion in 1 tablespoon olive oil until soft and browned (about 15 minutes). Place the tomatillos, garlic, onion, and remaining ingredients (except lime juice) in a blender. Blend until combined; consistency should be even, with no lumps. Add water if necessary. Add lime juice and blend for a few seconds.

For the beef, bring beef up to room-temperature, covered with plastic wrap. Season beef with salt and pepper. Heat olive oil in pan over high heat, then sauté beef over medium heat for 5 minutes each side. Soften tortillas in heated corn oil and set aside.

To serve, place a tortilla on a plate and place the beef on the tortilla. Put the cheese on top of the beef and place under the broiler until the cheese melts. Surround the beef with about 3/4 cup of sauce per plate. Garnish beef by sprinkling with coarsely chopped cilantro.

BEEF WITH OYSTERS

(Serves 4)

Mark Miller

For the beef:
4 6-ounce Certified Angus Beef
  center-cut filets
Salt and pepper to taste
2 tablespoons virgin olive oil

For the Yucatan oysters:
20 to 24 fresh oysters
2 tablespoons black peppercorns
3 large cloves garlic, peeled
1/2 teaspoon salt
3 tablespoons olive oil
3 bay leaves
2 tablespoons fresh lime juice

For the leeks:
4 leeks (both green and white parts),
  cut into thin julienne strips
2 tablespoons unsalted butter
Salt and pepper to taste

For the sauce:
1 quart beef stock
1 tablespoon roasted cumin seeds,
  ground
1 tablespoon roasted dried thyme
6 cloves roasted garlic
1 cup Yucatan oysters, pureed
2 tablespoons unsalted butter

For the pico de gallo:
2 tablespoons diced onion
2 cups tomatoes, chopped into 1/4-
  inch cubes
2 serraño chiles, finely chopped
2 tablespoons finely chopped cilantro
2 teaspoons sugar
1/4 cup Mexican beer
2 teaspoons salt
Juice of 1 lime

For the garnish:
12 small oysters (such as Hogg
  Island or Crescent Bay)

For the beef, bring beef up to room
temperature, covered with plastic wrap.
Season beef with salt and pepper. Heat
oil in pan over high heat, then sauté
beef over medium heat for 5 minutes
each side.

For the Yucatan oysters, shuck
oysters and reserve juice. Put oyster
juice into a hot saute pan and bring to a
boil. Add oysters and poach gently for 2
to 3 minutes until their edges curl slightly. Put peppercorns, garlic and salt into
a mortar and grind to a rough paste.
Add 1/2 cup hot oyster juice to the mortar and continue to grind.

continued on page 66

RAIMUND HOFMEISTER

ntury
za Hotel
s Angeles,
lifornia

Raimund Hofmeister, executive chef of the Century Plaza Hotel in Los Angeles and soon-to-be director of the Southern California International Culinary Institute, believes in the practice of give and take.

"You have to give when you take," said Hofmeister, 40, Certified Master Chef who has built quite a culinary career on the West Coast he loves so dearly.

"Of all the places I have lived, none of them have been as exciting as Los Angeles. By the year 2000 you can expect LA to be the number one city in this country," predicted Hofmeister, a native of Germany who apprenticed in Baden-Baden and worked in some of Europe's finest hotels before coming to the United States.

That's why Hofmeister is driven to open a culinary school in the Anaheim area. "We on the West Coast need our own culinary school," he said. "I feel the teaching requirements are different here. We are a melting pot of cultures, and our population is greatly Asian and Hispanic."

For that reason Hofmeister hopes to offer language classes at the school in addition to real hands-on culinary experience. The large number of hotels in the Anaheim area alone would offer students a means of work after graduation and during the school year if they needed financial support.

Hofmeister is fortunate to have the support of the Westin hotel group in his endeavor. He may stay on board until all necessary financing has been arranged. Hofmeister is a longtime employee of the

Westin chain, joining them in 1972. He assisted in the opening of the Westin in Johannesburg, South Africa, then moved to Kansas City, Atlanta, Detroit, Maui, Tulsa and finally Los Angeles.

An energy-packed chef, Hofmeister supervises a crew of 140 cooks at the Century Plaza. The hotel does $2 million in food revenue per month, has four restaurants, 24-hour room service, a kosher kitchen and banquet facilities capable of serving 5,500 dinners. Because of the hotel's location and its reputation with Hofmeister at the helm, dignitaries often stay and dine at the Century Plaza. When past President Ronald Reagan is in the area, he makes a stop.

When away from the hotel, Hofmeister is either judging a food show along the West Coast or traveling as one of Westin's seven culinary coordinators. He is active in the American Culinary Federation (ACF) and has participated on the U.S. Culinary team and a regional ACF team at the Culinary Olympics in Frankfurt.

Hofmeister serves Certified Angus Beef in all the Century Plaza restaurants and considers the beef a "true product of quality."

exican Pepper Beef in Eggplant Pirogue

ecipe on page 66

TENDERLOIN OF BEEF "MESA VERDE"

(Serves 2)

For the beef:
2 8-ounce Certified Angus Beef
   tenderloin steaks
Salt and black pepper
Red pepper flakes
Dijon mustard

For the herbal topping:
6 tablespoons beef marrow
3 tablespoons diced shallots
Dash of ground or fresh grated ginger
1/4 cup or more fresh white bread
   crumbs
1 1/2 teaspoons Cajun seasoning
1/4 teaspoon fresh thyme
1 teaspoon chopped parsley
1 teaspoon chopped cilantro
2 teaspoons cut chives
Salt and pepper

For the black bean sauce:
2 pounds dry black beans
2 quarts cold chicken stock
1 quart water
4 cloves garlic
2 medium onions
2 medium tomatoes
6 strips bacon
1 1/2 cups chopped green onions
5 serrano chiles
1 bay leaf
1 tablespoon brown sugar
1 teaspoon ground cumin
1/2 teaspoon cayenne pepper
1 teaspoon dried oregano
1 bunch cilantro, chopped
Salt and white pepper to taste

For the goat cheese chiles relleños:
2 medium-sized Anaheim green chile
   peppers
6 ounces softened goat cheese
1 teaspoon chopped fresh thyme
1/3 cup all-purpose flour
2 eggs, beaten
2/3 cup cornmeal
Oil for frying

For the wildflower salsa:
3 tomatoes, chopped
1 medium onion, chopped
3 green onions, chopped
3 canned green chiles, chopped
1 fresh serrano chile, minced
Juice of 1 lemon
1/4 teaspoon minced garlic
1/2 teaspoon dried oregano
3 tablespoons coarsely chopped
   cilantro
16 nasturtiums, coarsely chopped
Salt and white pepper to taste

For the beef, season steaks with salt, pepper and pepper flakes and sauté on both sides in a hot skillet for about 2 minutes each. Remove from pan and brush the top of each medallion with Dijon mustard.

For the herbal topping, combine beef marrow, shallots, ginger, bread crumbs, Cajun seasoning, thyme, parsley, cilantro, chives and salt and pepper. Top medallions heavily with the herbal topping and gently press on and shape it nicely to an

even quarter inch. Put back into a skillet and finish in the oven to the desired temperature. Cut open with a knife halfway so the inside can be seen.

For the black bean sauce, in a large soup pot place beans, cold chicken stock and water. Put on high heat until boiling starts. Turn down to simmer. Cook covered approximately 25 minutes. Add garlic, onions, tomatoes, bacon, green onions, serrano chiles, bay leaf and cook covered until beans are soft. Add brown sugar, cumin, cayenne pepper, oregano and cilantro. Cook uncovered approximately 15 minutes. Season with salt and white pepper to taste. Remove from flame and let cool. Run through food processor until smooth.

For the goat cheese chiles relleños, place chiles over gas flame. Turn frequently and let skin blister evenly without burning. Place roasted chiles in plastic bag while still hot. Let sweat so the skin becomes easy to peel off - about 15 minutes. Peel skin off chiles and cool completely. Make a slit on top side of chile about 2 inches long. Remove as many seeds as possible. Combine softened goat cheese and thyme. Stuff this into each chile. Flour chiles lightly and dip in beaten egg. Roll in cornmeal. Fry in deep oil at 375 degrees F until golden brown.

For the wildflower salsa, combine tomatoes, onion, green onion, chiles, lemon juice, garlic, oregano, cilantro, nasturtiums and salt and pepper to taste.

To serve, place the steaks on plate with black bean sauce, chiles relleños and wildflower salsa.

OREAN STYLE BROILED SHORT RIBS

(rves 4)

For the marinade:
1/2 cup soy sauce
1/2 cup honey
3 tablespoons rice vinegar
2 tablespoons ginseng extract
1/2 teaspoon red pepper flakes
1/2 teaspoon minced garlic
1/2 teaspoon minced ginger
1/2 cup minced green onion
1/2 cup vegetable oil

For the garnish:
Deep-fried bok choy
Sautéed wood ear mushrooms
Dilled cucumber slices
Edible flowers

For the barbecue sauce:
1/4 cup soybean oil
2 cloves minced garlic
1/2 cup minced shallots
2 cups ketchup
1/4 cup rice vinegar
1/2 cup soy sauce
1 cup brown sugar
1 tablespoon dry mustard
1 teaspoon paprika
2 tablespoons lemon juice
1/2 cup pineapple juice
2 cups water

For the beef:
2 pounds Certified Angus Beef short
   ribs, thinly cut
Black sesame seeds

For the marinade, combine all ingredients. Pour marinade over the meat and keep it in the refrigerator a minimum of 6 hours or overnight.

For the beef, charbroil the ribs on both sides. Place them on a wire rack, brush with barbecue sauce and sprinkle with black sesame seeds. Put under a slow broiler or salamander for approximately 3 more minutes, then brush on sauce one more time before serving.

For the barbecue sauce, in a sauce pan sauté oil, garlic and shallots without giving any color, until soft. Add all remaining ingredients and simmer over low heat for 15 minutes. Adjust consistency with water.

To serve, place ribs and sauce on plate. Serve with breaded and deep-fried bok choy, sautéed wood ear mushrooms, dilled cucumbers and edible flower.

CHRISTIAN RASSINOUX

Ritz Carlton
Laguna Niguel
Laguna Niguel,
California

Christian Rassinoux is accustomed to the unexpected. And as executive chef of the Ritz Carlton Laguna Niguel in southern California, this means getting used to earthquakes that shake pots and pans from their racks and send sauces sailing onto the floor.

But more often than not, Rassinoux, 40, tries to please the steady crowd of guests who venture to one of the West Coast's most luxurious hotel properties, situated atop a 150-foot bluff overlooking the Pacific Ocean and Catalina Island.

Born in Paris, Rassinoux made his way to the United States in just the same fashion as so many European chefs - via a number of countries. He trained in the Paris hotel school, then worked in Switzerland and Singapore. From there

Rassinoux went to South Africa, Cope[n]hagen, Los Angeles and Ottawa with t[he] Westin Hotel Company before joining [the] Ritz Carlton.

Of all the venues in which the chef h[as] worked, he said Asia was his favorite. A[nd] he tries to incorporate these Eastern flavors on his menus. California has affected the Frenchman's style of cookin[g] too. In the hotel's Cafe a Fitness Cuisin[e] menu is offered. "I am much more care[ful] of what I eat now," Rassinoux said. "People are very health and fitness con[scious here."

But southern California isn't all nuts a[nd] berries. Rassinoux's staff prepares Cer[-]tified Angus Beef prime rib and steaks, and he said beef is as popular as ever.

SMOKED MEDALLIONS WITH RED PEPPER SAUCE

(Serves 4)

For the beef:
8 3-ounce Certified Angus Beef
  medallions, cut from the tenderloin
Oil or clarified butter for sauteing

For the pepper sauce:
4 tablespoons white wine
3/4 cup veal demi-glace
4 tablespoons pureed roasted red
  bell peppers
Salt and pepper to taste
2 tablespoons butter

For the garnish:
Julienne strips of red and green
  pepper
Diamonds of yellow pepper
Fresh sprigs of chervil

For the beef, smoke medallions in a medium-hot smoker with intense smoke for about 5 minutes. Then, sauté in oil or clarified butter on both sides to finish cooking. Set aside.

For the sauce, reduce white wine in saucepan by half. Add veal demi-glace and red pepper puree. Reduce slowly u[ntil] sauce comes to a nice consistency. Stra[in] into another pan, add salt and pepper, and whisk in butter.

To serve, pour sauce onto plates. Top with two medallions of beef per each plate. Arrange a fence of alternating pep[-]per strips around edge of sauce. Top wit[h] four diamonds of yellow pepper and garnish with chervil.

RI-TIP PROVENCAL

(rves 4 to 5)

For the provencal garnish:
2 tablespoons olive oil
2 slices bacon, cubed
1 small carrot, sliced
1/2 fennel bulb, minced
1 small bunch parsley with stems
10 black olives, crushed to remove pit
1 cup white wine, salt to taste
2 cups veal demi-glace

For the garnish:
Baby corn
Shredded carrots
Peas
Pearl onions, blanched

For the marinade, combine all ingredients and marinate the meat overnight.

The next day, remove the meat from the marinade and strain the liquid, keeping the solids and liquids separate.

In a hot pan with olive oil, sauté beef to a golden brown. Take the meat out and sauté all the solids from the marinade. Blanch the bacon in boiling water for 10 seconds. Place the bacon and beef back in the pan along with the carrot, fennel, parsley and olives. Add the marinade and the wine and reduce a few minutes. Add the veal demi-glace and cook for about 2 hours. Once the meat has cooked, take it out, then reduce the sauce by half.

To serve, slice meat and arrange on serving platter. Garnish with baby corn, shredded carrots, peas and pearl onions. Can be served with polenta or pasta.

For the beef and marinade:
3 pounds Certified Angus Beef
    bottom sirloin butt, tri-tip steak
1/2 cup white wine
1 tablespoon Cognac
2 tablespoons olive oil
1/4 cup chopped onions
2 garlic cloves, minced
1/2 orange, zested
10 peppercorns, 1 sprig lemon thyme

Stanford
Court
San
Francisco,
California

LAWRENCE VITO

When Larry Vito, executive chef of the Stanford Court Hotel in San Francisco, isn't in the kitchen he's outside sailing and skiing. Vito used to own a 28-foot sailboat when he was living in Martha's Vineyard, and now that he's settled on the West Coast the fine California weather offers the chef a year round opportunity for outdoor play.

That's if this chef of the Mobile five-star Stanford Court can get away from his two restaurants and banquets. "Working in the hotel is very exciting," Vito, 38, said. "It keeps me busy constantly."

Vito hasn't made his career in the hotels. "I don't have a hotel orientation to food. Often hotels have bad reputations when it comes to food," he said.

Vito was born on Long Island, N.Y., and

worked in the kitchen of a local resort, cook in college and then decided to become an English teacher, not chef. However, he switched back to cooking enough time to attend the Culinary Inst of America.

Prior to the Stanford Court he was ch at the Desert Cafe in Santa Fe. "Four y ago I wanted to live in San Francisco, a now I'm finally here."

Vito enjoys shopping at the farmers market in San Rafael. He purchases 35 ferent kinds of tomatoes, for example. V has also found that in San Francisco the true sourdough breads turn out much be ter "because of the wild yeasts in the air Whereas the dry, desert air in Santa Fe tended to retard the growth of sourdoug bacteria that give flavor to the food."

Grilled Filet Mignon with Rosemary Sauce

Recipe on page 73

AN FRANCISCO MARINATED TRI-TIP SALAD

(rves 4)

For the marinade:
12 ounces porter beer
1/2 cup soy sauce
2 teaspoons sugar
2 cloves garlic, minced
Juice of 1 lemon
1 tablespoon chopped fresh thyme
1/4 cup diced sweet onion
8 Shiitzu leaves, chopped
1 1/2 pounds Certified Angus Beef
    bottom sirloin butt, tri-tip

For the red pepper pesto:
10 red bell peppers, roasted, peeled
    and seeded
3 garlic cloves
3 tablespoons lightly toasted
    pine nuts
3 tablespoons Parmesan cheese,
    finely grated
4 to 5 tablespoons olive oil
Salt and pepper to taste

For the garnish:
1/2 cup (packed) julienne-sliced
    jicama
Washed fresh salad greens
Light vinaigrette

For the marinade, combine beer, soy sauce, sugar, garlic, lemon juice, thyme, onion and Shiitzu leaves. Pour over beef and refrigerate. Marinate for 2 to 3 days.

For the pesto, combine red peppers, garlic, pine nuts, Parmesan, olive oil and salt and pepper in blender or food processor. Puree.

To serve, remove meat from marinade and pat dry. Grill until rare. Slice and arrange on plate. Garnish with jicama, salad greens tossed with vinaigrette and top with pesto.

TOKYO STYLE TENDERLOIN WITH SEASONAL FRUITS AND VEGETABLES

(Serves 12)

For the beef:
1 5-pound Certified Angus Beef
   tenderloin
Salt and pepper

For the vinaigrette:
1 tablespoon minced onion
1 teaspoon Dijon mustard
Salt and pepper to taste
7 tablespoons wine vinegar
1 1/4 cups olive oil

For the Japanese sauce:
3 tablespoons grated daikon
2 tablespoons minced garlic
2 tablespoons grated horseradish
1 teaspoon grated fresh ginger
1 1/2 cups soy sauce
3/4 cup mirin
   (sweet sake)
3/4 cup water
Salt and pepper
   to taste

For the vegetables and fruits:
Strawberries
Yellow tomatoes
Cherry tomatoes
Rape blossoms
Okra, Cauliflower
Red chicory
Broccoli
Ornamental kale
Water chestnuts
Zucchini
Asparagus

For the garnish:
Pine needles
Fresh edible flowers

For the beef, remove fat and silver skin from meat. Cut meat into workable blocks. Rub with salt and pepper. Cook over a hot charcoal fire to sear outside. Remove meat from heat to keep rare to medium-rare. Place in freezer to quickly chill meat. After chilling, place beef in refrigerator until ready to slice and serve.

For the produce, wash fruits and crisp lettuces. Steam okra, rape blossoms, broccoli flowerets, cauliflower flowerets, zucchini and asparagus with a pinch of salt. Refresh and set aside.

For vinaigrette, place onion, mustard, salt and pepper in a mixing bowl. Whisk in vinegar and then whisk in oil, little by little.

For the Japanese sauce, place daikon, garlic, ginger and horseradish in bowl. Add soy sauce, mirin, water and salt and pepper to taste. Mix well.

To serve, slice beef into 1/8- to 1/4-inch slices. Place on serving plates with arrangement of fruits and vegetables. Serve both the vinaigrette and Japanese sauce for dipping. Garnish with pine needles and edible flowers.

TAKASHI WADA

New Tokyo Restaurant Co., Ltd.
Tokyo, Japan

Certified Angus Beef is a success story in Tokyo, where 45 units of the 200-unit New Tokyo restaurant group serve and promote the product.

Some 120 tons of Certified Angus Beef are sold per year at these restaurants across Japan that specialize in grilled beef and traditional Japanese dishes like sukiyaki, teriyaki and shabu-shabu.

Traditionally, highly marbled Japanese beer-fed Kobe or more costly Matsusaka beef has been thinly sliced and used in these preparations. The local beef is rich from the high fat content but very expensive for the average consumer to afford.

Certified Angus Beef is an alternative, and one that does not compromise flavor. Because of its high marbling, it can be used in traditional Japanese preparations.

And because the Japanese are always in pursuit of the top quality product, no matter the country of origin, they have found Certified Angus Beef to be an exceptional product. In Japan, a country that considers beef a special occasion food, beef consumption is on the rise, doubling in the past 20 years. And since it's impossible to raise much beef in the mountainous country, Japan is forced to import.

Naoe Hirota, president of the New Tokyo Restaurant Co., Ltd., and chef Takashi Wada like to present Certified Angus Beef as simply as possible. They sear the beef tenderloin, slice it thinly and serve it with dipping sauce of sake and soy sauce and various Japanese garnishes like fresh bamboo shoots.

ROULADE OF SIRLOIN WITH RED SKIN POTATO SALAD

Peter Loren

(Serves 4)
from page 46

For the marinade:
1 cup chicken stock
2 tablespoons sherry
1 tablespoon oyster sauce
2 tablespoons soy sauce
1 1/2 teaspoons sesame oil
1 1/2 teaspoons finely minced shallots
Pinch finely minced garlic
Pinch minced fresh ginger
1 1/2 teaspoons sesame seeds,
   toasted
2 teaspoons sugar, salt to taste

For the sauce:
Cornstarch and water as needed
   to thicken marinade

For the beef:
14 ounces Certified Angus Beef
   bottom sirloin butt, ball tip
3/4 cup sesame seeds
1 teaspoon coarsely ground black
   pepper
1 tablespoon sesame oil
1 tablespoon peanut oil

For the potato salad:
2 cups red skin potatoes, cooked
   and cut into 3/8-inch cubes
1/2 cup chopped red onions
1/2 cup finely chopped bok choy
1/2 cup mayonnaise
1/4 cup enoki mushrooms, cut into
   1/2-inch lengths
1/4 cup sliced shiitake mushrooms
1/4 cup sliced oyster mushrooms
1/4 cup chopped green onions

For the garnish:
8 1/8-inch thick red onion slices
Fresh chives
Shiitake, oyster and enoki mushrooms

For the marinade, combine chicken
stock, sherry, oyster sauce and soy
sauce. Simmer over low heat. Sauté s
lots, garlic, ginger and sesame seeds
sesame oil and add this to above mixt
Season with sugar and salt as needed

For the beef, marinate beef in Orien
marinade overnight. Cover meat with
sesame seeds and black pepper. Sear
sesame and peanut oils in a hot skillet
Remove meat and let rest.

For the salad, combine potatoes, rec
onions, bok choy, mayonnaise, mushrooms and green onions.

To serve, place two red onion slices
each plate. Slice beef and wrap slices
around 1 1/2 tablespoons potato salad
Set atop onion slices. Garnish plate wit
chives and mushrooms.

For sauce, strain and reheat marinac
Add enough cornstarch and water to th
en for sauce. Spoon sauce onto plate.

SAUTÉED FILET WITH CHASSEUR SAUCE

Jean Banchet
from page 51

For the garnish:
Fluted mushrooms
Assorted blanched and seasoned
   baby vegetables

For the beef, season with salt and pepper. Sauté filet in a hot pan with the
clarified butter and cook medium-rare.
Keep warm.

For the sauce, remove fat from the p
Add a little of fresh butter and the
chopped shallots. Cook for 1 minute. Ac
the chopped tomatoes and sauté for 1
minute. Add the sliced mushrooms and
the white wine and cook until reduced a
the way to syrup. Add the demi-glace a
cook until reduced to half. Remove from
heat and add the butter and chopped
tarragon. Season to taste with salt and
pepper.

For garnish and to serve, place beef
with sauce on plate and surround with
vegetables. Top with mushroom cap.

BEEF WITH OYSTERS

Mark Miller
from page 56

Remove oysters from sauté pan and
reserve. Add olive oil and bay leaves to liquid in pan and bring to a boil. Blend in mixture from mortar, remove from heat and
add lime juice. Pour this mixture over
oysters and puree in blender.

For the sauce, combine stock, thyme,
ground cumin seeds, garlic and the cup
of pureed oysters. Cook for 20 minutes
over low heat and then strain. Add 2
tablespoons of butter and incorporate.

For the leeks, cook in lightly salted
water for about 2 minutes. Drain carefully

and toss in 2 tablespoons butter, salt an
pepper to taste.

For the pico de gallo, put onion in a
strainer, rinse with hot water and drain.
Add all the ingredients and mix well. Let
sit in the refrigerator for at least 1/2 hour
before serving.

To serve, place the sauce on a large
dinner plate, and the beef in the center,
on the sauce. On each plate, divide leeks
into 3 portions around the beef and plac
an oyster on top of each leek portion (3
per plate). Garnish with pico de gallo

MEXICAN PEPPER BEEF IN EGGPLANT PIROGUE

Raimund Hofmeister
from page 57

For the pirogues:
1 medium eggplant
1 cup fresh white bread crumbs
1/2 teaspoon red pepper flakes
1 teaspoon Cajun seasoning
Salt and pepper
1 egg
4 tablespoons all-purpose flour

For the pepper beef:
3 tablespoons sunflower oil
1 pound cubed lean Certified Angus
   Beef (chuck or top sirloin)
Salt and pepper
2 tablespoons butter
1/2 teaspoon garlic, minced
1/2 teaspoon Cajun seasoning
1 teaspoon paprika
1 teaspoon chili powder
1/2 teaspoon red pepper flakes
2 cups beef stock
1/3 cup pearl onions
1 small red bell pepper, seeded,
   cored and diced
1 small green bell pepper, seeded,
   cored and diced
1/3 cup mushrooms
1/2 cup heavy cream

For the garnish:
Steamed and buttered carrots and
   a timbale of wild and white rice

For pirogues, peel and cut eggplant in
half and hollow the inside out. Mix bread
crumbs with flaked red pepper, Cajun
spice, salt and pepper. In a separate bow
crack one egg and beat with 3 to 4
tablespoons of water. Now dust the
eggplant with flour, dip into the egg and
then roll in the bread crumbs. Press the
breading lightly.

For the pepper beef, preheat large skill
and add oil. When pan is very hot, sauté
beef cubes quickly to a brown color.
Season with salt and pepper. Put into a
sieve to drain off all grease and keep to th
side. In a separate casserole, melt butter,
add garlic, Cajun spice, paprika, chili powder and flaked red pepper. Heat lightly to i
tensify color, then add some beef stock
and reduce by half. In the meantime, put
pearl onions, peppers and mushrooms in a
hot pan. Brown off lightly, put together with
the meat and mix with the sauce. Bring to
quick boil. add the cream. To serve, deep-
fry the eggplant and serve pepper beef in i

The Great American Steakhouse

Edd Hendee, owner of Taste of Texas in Houston, satisfies hungry patrons by cutting Certified Angus Beef steaks to order.

Whether it's situated in a bustling East Coast seaport or in a conservative Midwestern town, the steakhouse remains the classic of American restaurants.

There is something simple and sacred about a perfectly cooked steak and accoutrements like fried onion rings and stuffed potatoes. While every steakhouse may sauce the steak a bit differently and offer its version of the side dishes, steakhouses are the same in that they are dear to American diners. Even consumers who have snubbed beef in fear of cholesterol haven't seemed to affect the popularity of these bastions of 32-ounce T-bones. The steakhouse just transcends time.

As we move into the 1990s, the steakhouse will attract even more quality-conscious consumers who may eat less red meat at home but want to order a fine steak when they dine out.

Ask the owners, managers and chefs of these restaurants, and they will tell you the most important reason steakhouses enjoy continued success is that the meal, invariably, tastes good. High quality of the steak is imperative, and there's no better tasting or dependable product to serve in a steakhouse than Certified Angus Beef. In fact, many steakhouse operators totally commit to Certified Angus Beef, putting the federally registered Certified Angus Beef trademark on their menu to tell their customers they proudly serve the world's finest beef.

Edd C. Hendee opted to go this route at his **Taste of Texas** steakhouse in Houston, the country's largest volume single-unit Certified Angus Beef restaurant, which does 3,700 covers a week.

Hendee has been in the restaurant business for 19 years, but it wasn't until the last 5 years when he focused his efforts on top-quality beef and joined the Certified Angus Beef Program, that his venture has been really successful.

"I had tried other beef before Certified Angus Beef, but it was very inconsistent. Our restaurant wasn't successful; it was mediocre at best. We were just ecstatic to find a consistent product like Certified Angus Beef so we could specialize in steaks. During the past 4 years my sales have almost tripled," Hendee said. He buys some 5,500 to 6,000 pounds of Certified Angus Beef monthly. And for a typical month, 180 Certified Angus Beef carcasses are needed just to fill the restaurant's most popular order - prime rib.

Hendee said a hurdle for him to overcome was that Texas is synonymous with beef, but Texas "means so much to so many different people. Texans eat more beef per capita than residents of any other U.S. state. 'The bigger the better' they always say here," Hendee said, "but in the end, quality is more important than quantity." Taste of Texas carries out the Lone Star State theme by offering side dishes of fried okra, sautéed sweet onions and tortilla soup with its steaks. You'll find that the items on the menu as well as the paintings on the walls add to the overall atmosphere of a steakhouse.

Memorabilia like armadillos and the flag of the Lone Star State add to the Texas motif at the casual Taste of Texas restaurant in Houston.

The Great American Steakhouse

Traditionally, steakhouses have had dark, heavy surroundings with comfortable, oversized chairs that appealed primarily to business clientele, the majority of whom were male. But with steak's mass appeal, modern steakhouse operators are targeting a broader-based, more casual audience with lighter surroundings.

Surroundings at Babe's Steakhouse in Philadelphia are a change of pace, and in addition to serving Certified Angus Beef steaks cooked over charcoal, the restaurant offers a raw seafood bar, music from the 1930s and 40s and a moving dance floor.

The surroundings at **Babe's Steakhouse** on Aramingo Avenue in Philadelphia were certainly a change of pace for steakhouses. Set in an old warehouse in a neighborhood where owner and millionaire developer Frederick "Babe" Kozlowski's family has lived for more than 150 years, the restaurant serves Certified Angus Beef to the business crowd at lunch and to those folks who come to Babe's for purely social reasons for dinner, said executive chef and director of operations Raymond Bertschy.

While the steaks are certainly why many people frequent Babe's, the atmosphere is a drawing card. Music from the 1930s and 40s is played live from a moving dance floor. A glass elevator transports guests between floors. An observation grill downstairs is where the chefs cook steaks over gas-fired charcoal. And diners can relax on black leather sofas and nosh on crab, oysters, clams, lobster and Beluga caviar from the raw bar.

"Dining is really entertainment here," Bertschy said. Babe's is an atmosphere-pumped steakhouse/show palace with something for everyone. "We're above the average steakhouse," he said, "because of the atmosphere and because we're the only steakhouse in town offering just Certified Angus Beef."

Yet, there is no disputing that business is still conducted in a steakhouse - always has been and always will be. Just like the no-nonsense food that is served, the conversation is usually very direct.

At lunch time at **John Q's Public Bar & Grille** on Public Square in Cleveland, Ohio, the majority of the patrons take care of business matters over their meal. That percentage drops to about 50 percent at dinner. John Q's is owned by Stouffer's, and Rick Cassara, Stouffer's vice president for marketing, said John Q's is "the perfect backdrop for business conversation because there is plenty of room, private booths and oversized chairs. The customer's time is his own," Cassara said.

John Q's, which is positioning itself as the city's premier steakhouse, is selling just Certified Angus Beef. The restaurant offers Certified Angus Beef New York strip, black peppered strip, top sirloin, filet mignon, porterhouse, Delmonico and prime rib. Waiters approach the table with various cuts of meat on silver trays for the diners to make their selections. All steaks are served with a choice of garlic butter, horseradish butter, Cognac/mustard sauce or Bearnaise sauce.

John Q's Public Bar & Grille, Cleveland's premier steakhouse, serves only Certified Angus Beef.

Side dishes include linguine with marinara sauce, sautéed mushrooms with Madeira and fried onion rings.

Steak continues to be the all-American food, especially in the eye of the foreigner. Although Certified Angus Beef is served in many other countries, most visitors like to partake of the product while visiting the United States.

Millionaire developer "Babe" Kozlowski built his steakhouse in an old warehouse in Philadelphia.

ne steakhouse that receives
y foreign visitors is **Scotch 'n Sir-**
on North Washington Street in
ton. "We get our share of
anese customers, that's for sure,"
Harry Johnson, owner and
eral manager. "The Japanese
w and appreciate quality in beef.
ton is an area high in technology,
an estimated 250,000 Japanese
inessmen and tourists come to
city each year," Johnson said.

"It's great seeing Larry Bird and
other Celtics enjoying Certified Angus
Beef steaks," Johnson said. Scotch 'n
Sirloin has been part of the Certified
Angus Beef Program for three
years.

In Kansas City, where **Plaza III** restaurant has been open in the Country
Club Plaza for more than 25 years,
the steakhouse concept is relatively
new. Only since 1986 has the restaurant been specializing in beef,

*Steve May of Creative Restaurant
Management, owner of Plaza III, says
the steakhouse customer is willing to
pay for top quality.*

from all over. Plaza III is still a special
occasion restaurant, and it brings in
the wealthy and business people
from all over the country, but now our
emphasis is on steaks."

Plaza III has the look of a classic
steakhouse - dark wood, black
leather, tufted booths and Western
art. May believes his company's in-
vestment in the concept was a good
one. "The steakhouse is here to stay
because people enjoy red meat, and
they're going to opt for the best steak
they can buy."

The future looks bright for Certified
Angus Beef, for American steakhouses and for the consumer who is
searching for a quality steak dinner.
Kozlowski and Bertschy hope to
open 5 or 6 more Babe's steakhouses around the country.

And in the words of Stouffer's Cassara: "In marketing I need to pay attention to people's habits. I have
found that while people may be
giving up red meat at home, when
they go out to a restaurant they want
a good steak."

They want a great steak - tender,
juicy and flavorful every time - and
that's Certified Angus Beef.

cotch 'n Sirloin is located in a renovated factory building near Boston Garden.

Extremely popular among Bos-
onians for more than 15 years,
cotch 'n Sirloin is located on the
ighth floor of an old factory building
ear Boston Garden. The restaurant
well known as a spot where sports
ans and celebrities gather before
nd after Celtics or Bruins games.
hey come for the atmosphere (the
nenu is printed on black lunch
oxes). And they come for the beef.

specifically Certified Angus Beef.

"We weren't doing as well as we
would have liked," said Steve May of
Creative Restaurant Management,
owner of Plaza III. "We felt that Kansas City needed an upscale steakhouse that would draw customers

*At Scotch 'n Sirloin in Boston owners
Orland Garwood and Harry Johnson
(seated) serve Certified Angus Beef to
fans before and after Celtics and
Bruins games.*

*Plaza III is a white tablecloth steakhouse in Kansas City, attracting business clien-
tele from across the country.*

PAUL BOCUSE

PAUL BOCUSE

Paul Bocuse
Restaurant
Collonges-au-
Mont d'Or,
France

The formidable, globetrotting Paul Bocuse has been a driving force in the food community and an ambassador of nouvelle cuisine around the world.

Born in the Lyonnaise region, and the son of a chef, Bocuse is known for his Romanesque features, his strong-as-steel personality and his restaurant called Paul Bocuse, located 15 minutes from the center of Lyon in Collonges- au- Mont d'Or, where bourgeois foods indigenous to the area are showcased.

It was many years ago that a young Bocuse apprenticed with the master Fernand Point in Vienne, did stints at Maxim's and Lucas-Carton, and then took over his father's restaurant in the 1950s. The bistro where Bocuse's father cooked simple foods is located just 100 yards from where Bocuse's world-famous establishment is situated today.

While his father was beloved by locals, Bocuse is a multi-country entrepreneur. His signature dishes of truffle soup topped with puff pastry, chicken poached in a bladder and garlic sausage wrapped and baked in brioche have withstood the test of time. He has endorsed products as varied as Beaujolais and the airlines. And the chef's influences have been felt in the United States, too.

In 1983 he and fellow French chefs Roger Verge and Gaston Lenotre opened the Chefs de France restaurant in Epcot Center in central Florida. Here they have duplicated French bistro cooking (Boeuf Bourguignonne, escargots, etc.) in a French pavilion complete with mock Eiffel Tower, bridge across a simulated Seine River and sidewalk cafe.

Bocuse's restaurant has enjoyed a Michelin three-star status for about 30 years, and Bocuse was awarded a Legion of Honor by then French President Valery Giscard d'Estaing in 1975. And at the awards meal afterward, Bocuse served the president his famous truffle soup.

BEEF ON A STRING

(Serves 6)

For the beef:
4 pounds Certified Angus Beef filet
1/2 pound carrots, cut into sticks
1/2 pound turnips, cut into sticks
6 leeks, white part only
2 celery hearts
3 tomatoes, peeled, seeded and quartered
1 onion, stuck with 3 cloves
1 sprig each parsley, chervil and tarragon
2 tablespoons coarse salt
1 teaspoon black peppercorns
2 tablespoons butter

For the garnish:
Croutons
Grated Parmesan cheese

For the beef, trim and tie filet.

For the remainder, heat 3 quarts of water in a large soup pot, adding the vegetables and seasonings. After 5 minutes of boiling, plunge in the beef, tied by a string to the handle of the kettle; this will help in removing the meat. After skimming well, continue to cook at a gentle boil. Allow 10 to 15 minutes for each pound; as for roast beef, the meat should remain rosy red inside.

Serve the meat surrounded by the vegetables and accompanied by tomato sauce seasoned with tarragon and chives; you can also serve the meat simply with coarse salt, cornichons, and small pickled onions. It can also be eaten with a remoulade sauce. After lightly buttering the broth, serve it with small bread croutons and grated Parmesan cheese.

CHARLES CARROLL

CURED FLANK STEAK WITH SPICY SHRIMP

(Serves 1)

Balsam's
Grand Resort
Dixville Notch,
New
Hampshire

For the curing:
1 gallon water
1 cup liquid hickory smoke
1 tablespoon curing salt

For the beef:
6 ounces Certified Angus Beef flank steak, butterflied
3 Spanish shrimp (2 for garnish)
1/4 cup green bell pepper
1/4 cup red bell pepper
2 ounces flank trim (ground)
Garlic, paprika
Thyme
Salt and pepper to taste
Hot pepper sauce

For the garnish:
1/2 cup julienned carrots, blanched
1/3 cup julienned leeks, blanched
1/2 cup bechamel sauce (recipe on page 78)
1 egg
Fresh Parmesan cheese on top

For the sauce:
1 cup red wine
2 shallots, minced
1 clove garlic, minced
2 cups veal demi-glace
1 tablespoon fresh tarragon
2 tablespoons tomato concasse
Salt and pepper to taste

For the curing, combine all ingredients and allow flank steak to sit overnight.

For the beef, lay out the flank steak. Small dice 1 shrimp. Mix with peppers and ground flank, plus seasonings. Place stuffing on top and roll up. Tie the meat. Roast at 375 degrees F.to an internal temperature of 120 degrees. Let rest for 30 minutes.

For the garnish, grease ramekin. Place half of the vegetables in the dish. Mix egg with bechamel sauce and pour on top. Finish with cheese. Bake at 350 to 375 degrees until hot. Deep-fry remaining vegetables.

For the sauce, place wine, shallots and garlic in a saucepan. Reduce to a glaze. Add demi-glace, tarragon and tomato, and reduce by half. Strain and season to taste.

SPINACH WRAPPED EYE OF ROUND

(Serves 4)

For the beef:
1 small Certified Angus Beef eye of round, trimmed
1 pound spinach, fresh basil
2 cups mushrooms, 2 egg whites
1 clove garlic, minced
1/4 cup pine nuts, toasted
6 ounces trimmed Certified Angus Beef flank, ground
1 tablespoon vegetable oil
Salt and pepper to taste
1 sheet caul fat

For the sauce:
Beurre blanc, pesto sauce

For the ratatouille:
1/2 eggplant
1 tomato, peeled, seeded and diced
1 zucchini, diced, 1 squash, diced
1 onion, diced
4 tablespoons olive oil
2 tablespoons minced garlic
2 tablespoons chopped cilantro
Salt and pepper to taste

For the fried eggplant:
1/2 eggplant
Flour, egg wash

For the beef, trim the eye of round down; use trimming for stuffing. Put spinach, mushrooms, garlic and pine nuts in a food processor and pulse. Sauté mixture in a little oil and drain well. Cool and mix with ground flank, basil, salt, pepper, egg whites and reserved ground trimmings. Lay caul fat down, top with a 1/2 inch layer of mixture and the eye of round. Roll up and tie. Bake at 375 degrees F until 120 degrees internal temperature. Let rest for 30 minutes.

For the ratatouille, chop the eggplant, add to other vegetables and sauté in olive oil until very soft. Add garlic, cilantro and salt and pepper to taste. For the fried eggplant, slice thin and dip in flour and egg wash. Either broil or fry until crisp on both sides. To serve, slice beef and serve with ratatouille, fried eggplant slices and sauce of pesto-enhanced beurre blanc.

AYMOND BERTSCHY

OACHED TENDERLOIN IN BEEF BROTH WITH FRESH HERBS AND VEGETABLES

(erves 2)

abe's
teakhouse
hiladelphia,
ennsylvania

For the beef:
2 cups beef consomme
2 6-ounce Certified Angus Beef
    tenderloin steaks
6 asparagus spears
10 carrot sticks, julienned
2 sprigs fresh thyme
2 tablespoons butter

For the beef, bring consomme to a boil in saucepan and add beef. Reduce heat to a simmer. Poach beef until desired doneness; then remove and keep warm. In the same pan, place asparagus, carrot sticks and thyme, and cook until al dente. Keep warm.

For the sauce, reduce 3/4 cup of consomme until half its volume. Add butter to consomme, whisking. Then simmer slightly. Slice each tenderloin and shingle onto serving plate. Arrange vegetables and thyme around each portion. Coat with sauce and serve.

ARTHUR MANGIE

FILET OF BEEF WITH PARMESAN SAUCE

(Serves 4)

ittsburgh
National Bank
ittsburgh,
Pennsylvania

For the garnish:
Ricotta cheese
Ground peppercorns
Roasted Peppers
Chopped garlic, olive oil
Chopped green onions
Italian parsley leaves

For the sauce:
2 large shallots
1/4 teaspoon minced parsley
1 egg yolk
1/2 cup freshly grated Parmesan
    cheese
2 tablespoons Dijon mustard
1 tablespoon finely chopped garlic
1 tablespoon Worcestershire sauce
1/2 teaspoon fresh ground pepper
1/4 cup wine (red or white or
    combination of both)
3/4 cup olive oil

For the beef:
1 16 to 20-ounce Certified Angus
    Beef filet
1 tablespoon olive oil
1 teaspoon pureed fresh ginger
1 teaspoon minced fresh garlic
1 teaspoon cracked black pepper
    (or ground from pepper mill)
Salt to taste

For the beef, rub down filet with olive oil. Rub in fresh ginger and garlic. Sprinkle on pepper and lightly dust with salt. Filet can be charred on grill or in heavy skillet. Remember wherever it is done, don't overcook the beef. After it had been cooked, chill for 1 to 2 hours. Slice thin and arrange on plate.

For the sauce, place all ingredients in blender or food processor, except oil. Process until smooth. Gradually add oil until mixture is creamy.

Serve beef with a spoonful of ricotta cheese topped with ground peppercorns, and roasted peppers that are tossed in olive oil and chopped garlic. Scatter chopped green onions on beef, and garnish plate with Italian parsley leaves. Serve sauce to the side.

DAVID SPADAFORE

ROLLED FLANK STEAK SOUTHWESTERN STYLE

(Serves 4)

The Erie Club
Erie,
Pennsylvania

For the sauce:
1 1/2 tomatoes, peeled
2 tablespoons chopped onion
1 tablespoon chopped jalapeño
    pepper
2 tablespoons pickle relish

For the beef:
1 2-pound Certified Angus Beef
    flank steak
6 tablespoons kidney beans
6 tablespoons refried beans

For the garnish:
4 green onions
4 6-inch tortilla shells
1 cup avocado, chopped
12 red pepper strips (fresh or canned)
4 ounces Cheddar cheese, sliced
1 cup picante sauce

For the sauce, take peeled tomato, onion, jalapeño pepper and pickle relish, and place in blender and puree.

For the beef, with a boning knife, carefully cut flank steak in half by slicing meat thinly through the narrow end of the meat and continuing through to the other side, leaving a small piece of meat holding the two pieces together. Lay out and tenderize with meat hammer, then take cooked kidney beans and refried pinto beans and spread thin over meat. Roll and tie. Roast for 40 minutes in oven at 350 degrees F, then let cool. Thinly slice 1/4-inch in thickness with slicing knife.

For the garnish, first take green onions and char-broil over grill. Fry tortilla shells in french fryer. Then arrange avocado, red pepper strips, cheddar cheese, green onions and tortilla shell on serving plate, and place beef roll on top. Serve with picante sauce.

WALTER MEYER

BRAISED BEEF PIEMONTESE STYLE

(Serves 10)

Walt Disney
World Resort
Orlando,
Florida

For the beef:
4 1/2 pounds Certified Angus Beef
  sirloin, round, chuck or short ribs
5 ounces larding bacon
3 1/2 tablespoons beef fat or oil
1 cup mirepoix
1/4 cup bacon trimmings
3 1/2 tablespoons tomato puree
2 teaspoons salt
1/2 teaspoon pepper
1 cup red wine
1 quart beef stock
1 tablespoon cornstarch
1/4 cup Madeira

For the beef, lard the meat with strips of bacon. Brown meat in melted fat. Brown mirepoix and bacon trimmings. Add the tomato puree, salt and pepper. Deglaze the meat with the red wine. Reduce the liquid until it is a syrupy consistency. Add the beef stock. Cover the pan and braise the meat until tender. Turn occasionally. Remove the meat from the pan. Reduce the sauce to the described consistency or, if needed, bind with cornstarch. Strain and skim the fat. Add the Madeira wine. Pour a small quantity of sauce over the carved meat before serving.

STRIP LOIN STEAK IN THREE MUSTARD SAUCE

(Serves 2)

For the strip loin:
2 10-ounce boneless Certified Angus
  Beef strip loin steaks
Salt and pepper to taste
2 tablespoons clarified butter
1 tablespoon minced shallots
1/2 cup white wine
2 cups heavy cream
1/4 cup glace de viande
1 teaspoon Dijon mustard
1 teaspoon Meaux mustard
1 teaspoon Düsseldorf mustard
1 tablespoon chopped parsley
1 teaspoon chopped chives
1 tablespoon chopped fresh tarragon

For the garnish:
Sautéed mushrooms caps
Seasonal fresh vegetables
Sprigs of chives and tarragon

For the beef, season the steaks with salt and pepper. Heat 1 tablespoon of butter in a skillet. Sauté steaks on both sides until medium-rare and keep them warm in a 150 degree F oven. Pour off excess fat from the pan and lower the heat. Add remaining butter and shallots. Sauté until lightly brown, about 5 minutes. Add the white wine and reduce until all liquors have evaporated. Add cream and reduce

by a third. Add the glace de viande and simmer. Remove pan from the heat, add the mustards and herbs, and stir to blend. Taste for seasoning. Garnish the steaks with sautéed mushrooms caps, seasonal fresh vegetables and sprigs of chives and tarragon.

GERALD MESSERLI

MARINATED BEEF SKEWER FLAMBÉ

(Serves 4)

® Cerromar
Beach Hotel
Dorado,
Puerto Rico

For the beef:
2 pounds Certified Angus Beef
  tenderloin
4 pineapple boats
8 tablespoons dark rum

For the marinade:
3/4 cup soy sauce
1/4 cup brown sugar
3 tablespoons whiskey
3 tablespoons sesame oil
1 tablespoon grated ginger

For the sauce:
1/2 cup red wine vinegar
3 cups sherry
4 tablespoons English mustard
1 cup guava jelly
1/2 cup grated horseradish
1/2 cup tomato sauce
1 jalapeño pepper, chopped

For the garnish:
1 cup garlic, roasted
1/2 cup shallots, roasted

For the marinade, combine all ingredients and mix well. For the beef, cut in 1 inch cubes and marinate the beef in marinade overnight. Remove from the marinade and pat dry. Place on skewers and sear under broiler. For the sauce, combine all ingredients and mix well.

For the dish, place skewer in pineapple boat and flame with 158 proof dark rum (2 tablespoons each boat). Garnish with roasted garlic and shallots. Sauce is served on the side.

ROASTED FLANK STEAK WITH ORANGE SAUCE

(Serves 3)

For the meat:
1 pound Certified Angus Beef flank
  steak, butterflied
Salt and pepper to taste
1 teaspoon Caribbean jerk spice
3 ripe plantains, sliced and fried
1 cup blanched fresh spinach leaves
4 ounces beef fat

For the beef, season the meat with salt, pepper and jerk seasoning. Place fat back, plantains and spinach on top of meat. Roll up the meat, tie with string and roast at 500 degrees F for 25 minutes. Let rest 8 to 10 minutes before slicing.

For the sauce, mix all ingredients together and serve with beef.

For the sauce:
4 tablespoons butter
3 shallots, minced, salt & pepper
Pinch of cardamon
2 tablespoons brandy
1 tablespoon English mustard
1/2 cup minced orange
1/2 teaspoon jerk seasoning
3 cups beef stock

OHN FARNSWORTH

NEAPPLE SMOKED LOIN OF BEEF WITH HIBISCUS AIOLI

erves 6)

NEEL BAY

aneel Bay
t. John's,
.S. Virgin
lands

For the beef:
Skins from 10 pineapples
4 pounds Certified Angus Beef
   strip loin

For the dry cure mixture:
1 cup kosher salt
1 cup dark brown sugar
2 tablespoons whole black
   peppercorns, crushed
2 tablespoons whole coriander,
   crushed
1/2 teaspoon onion powder
1/2 teaspoon garlic powder
1/4 teaspoon coarse salt
1/2 teaspoon whole allspice, crushed
1/2 teaspoon whole clove, crushed

For the hibiscus aioli:
20 hibiscus flowers
2 tablespoons garlic, blanched
1/2 teaspoon salt
3 egg yolks
Juice from 2 lemons
2 cups extra virgin olive oil

For the pineapple salad:
1 1/2 cups pineapple, cut in
   1/4-inch dice
1/4 cup carrot, cut in 1/4-inch dice
1/4 cup celery, cut in 1/4-inch dice
1 tablespoon cilantro, minced
1/4 cup extra virgin olive oil
Juice from 1 lemon
Salt and cayenne pepper

One week before, dry the pineapple skins in an oven, set at the lowest temperature until thoroughly dried. Rough chop in food processor.

For the beef, mix all dry cure ingredients together. Remove fat and silver skin from strip loin. Place the meat into a stainless steel pan, rub with dry cure, cover and refrigerate for 48 hours.

To smoke beef, place dried pineapple in your smoker, and smoke the cured strip loin until an internal temperature of 115 degrees is reached. Remove and when cool, refrigerate.

For the aioli, in a mortar, pound the hibiscus flowers, garlic and salt into a paste. Add the egg yolks and lemon juice, and slowly whip in the olive oil until all is incorporated.

For the pineapple salad, mix all ingredients thoroughly and refrigerate.

To serve, slice meat very thin and lay out 5 pieces on a plate. Garnish with a 1/2 cup of the pineapple salad and three hibiscus petals. Pass the aioli separately.

EEF ON A LEEK WITH DARK RUM VINAIGRETTE AND PUMPKIN ZUCCHINI POLENTA

Serves 6)

For the polenta:
2 1/2 cups chicken stock
1/4 teaspoon garlic, minced
3/4 cup raw pumpkin, shredded
3/4 cup stone-ground cornmeal
1/2 cup zucchini, shredded
Salt and pepper

For the vinaigrette:
1 cup olive oil
1/2 cup dark rum
1/2 cup balsamic vinegar
2 tablespoons leek, blanched and
   minced
1/2 teaspoon tarragon, minced
1/2 teaspoon basil, minced
1/2 teaspoon oregano, minced
Salt and fresh ground pepper
2 quarts beef stock

For the beef:
6 6-ounce Certified Angus Beef
   tenderloin tails, chain and fat
   removed
24 pieces leek ribbons (1/4- by
   7 inches), blanched

For the polenta, the day before, bring to a boil the chicken stock, minced garlic and pumpkin. Add the cornmeal, whisking continuously. Lower the heat and cook until cornmeal leaves the sides of the pot. Fold in the zucchini and check the seasoning for salt and pepper. Place the polenta in 3 oiled U-shaped molds (5 3/8 inches by 1 1/2 inches). Chill overnight.

For the beef, tie each tenderloin tail 4 times with a leek ribbon leaving equal spacing between ties.

For the vinaigrette, mix together all the ingredients through the salt and pepper.

Place the beef stock in a pot and bring up to 190 degrees. Remove polenta from molds and cut in half crosswise. Place on a sheet pan and heat through in a 350 degree F oven. Place tenderloin tails in the stock and poach for 6 minutes. Remove and allow to rest 4 minutes, keeping them warm at the same time. Take 1 cup of the poaching liquor and add to the vinaigrette.

To serve, cut 3 3/8-inch slices from the polenta. Cut the tenderloin tails 3 times between

vinaigrette on a plate, arrange tenderloin on left side of plate in a straight line, the polenta on the right side of the plate. Start with the large piece of polenta first, then shingle the 3 3/8-inch slices towards you.

GRILLED FILET MIGNON WITH ROSEMARY SAUCE

Serves 4)

from page 62

**LAWRENCE
VITO**

For the vegetable mélange:
1 tablespoon olive oil
1 small onion, diced
6 baby artichokes, blanched and
   quartered
7 Kalamata olives, quartered
4 red cherry tomatoes, quartered
4 yellow cherry tomatoes, quartered
1 teaspoon fresh oregano, chopped
Salt and freshly ground pepper

For the polenta:
3 cups water
1 cup stone-ground yellow cornmeal
1 tablespoon grated Parmesan
   cheese
1 tablespoon olive oil
Salt and pepper to taste

For the beef:
4 10-ounce Certified Angus Beef
   filet mignons
1/4 cup olive oil, salt and pepper

For the rosemary sauce:
3 fresh sprigs rosemary, stripped
2 fresh sprigs thyme, stripped
3 bay leaves, 8 peppercorns
8 ounces beef shank, trimmed of fat
2 tablespoons olive oil
1 onion, chopped, 1 carrot, chopped
1 tomato, chopped
8 garlic cloves, chopped
2 cups white wine, 1 quart veal stock

For the vegetable mélange, heat a small pan over medium heat. Add the oil and gently saute the onions until translucent. Add the cooked baby artichokes, olives, tomatoes, and oregano. Sauté briefly until heated thoroughly. Season to taste with salt and pepper. Set aside.

For the polenta, mix 1 cup of water with cornmeal. Allow to stand 20 minutes. Combine the remainder of the water with the cornmeal in a heavy bottomed pot. Stir with a wooden spoon for 20 minutes over low heat. Add the Parmesan cheese and

salt and pepper to taste. In a baking dish, spread the mixture evenly, 1/2-inch thick. Allow to cool. The consistency should be dense and very firm with no lumps. Refrigerate. When cold cut into 3-inch squares. Set aside until final assembly.

For the beef, brush meat with oil and season on both sides with salt and pepper. Grill the meat quickly for 2 to 3 minutes per side for rare to medium-rare.

For the rosemary sauce, tie the rosemary, thyme, bay leaves and peppercorns in cheesecloth sachet. Sauté shank in olive oil until brown, add onion and carrot and continue browning. Add the tomatoes, sachet, garlic and wine and reduce until almost dry. Add stock, reduce on a low flame. Add 2 more sprigs of chopped rosemary. Allow to steep 5 minutes. Strain, and season with salt and pepper. The sauce should be the weight of heavy maple syrup and have a deep, rich, flavor.

Just after grilling the beef, brush the polenta squares with olive oil and grill on both sides. Allow the beef to rest while reheating the vegetables. To serve, place on warm serving plates.

TELL ERHARDT

CAYMAN STYLE TOP ROUND BARBECUE

(Serves 12)

Grand Old
House
Grand
Cayman
Island, British
West Indies

For the sauce:
Grated peel of 1 orange
Grated peel of 1 lemon
1/4 cup vinegar
1/4 cup vegetable oil
1/2 cup ketchup
1/2 cup honey
1/4 cup blackstrap molasses
1/4 cup chopped onion
Juice of 1 orange
Juice of 1 lemon
Pinch of salt

For the garnish:
Orange halves and parsley

For the beef:
4 to 5 pounds Certified Angus Beef
top round
6 cloves garlic, peeled
2 Scotch bonnet peppers, or jalapeño
peppers
Salt and pepper to taste
1/2 cup vegetable oil

For the sauce, combine the grated orange and lemon peels, vinegar, oil, ketchup, honey, molasses, onion, orange and lemon juices, and the salt in a saucepan. Bring to a boil and cook for 15 to 20 minutes, or until the sauce is reduced by half. (The color will change from light to dark red as the sauce cooks.)

For the beef, with a knife, prick the top round and insert the garlic and the peppers into the meat. You don't have to follow a pattern, but make sure it is equally distributed. Cover with the oil, turn once awhile and marinate overnight. Place the beef on the grill and cook slowly for approximately 1 1/2 to 2 hours or until desired doneness. Then brush with some of the sauce, let sit for 15 minutes and slice.

Garnish with orange halves and parsley. Serve with callaloo and corn bread. The reason for letting the beef sit for 15 minutes before slicing is so that a the juices can settle and nothing will run out of the roast when you make the first cut. (Callaloo is a Cayman style spinach but you can use whatever you like.)

GRILLED MARINATED SKIRT STEAK

(Serves 2)

For the marinade:
8 cloves garlic, minced
2 tablespoons ginger, diced
1 cup soy sauce
1/2 cup fresh squeezed lime juice
1/2 cup honey
Black pepper to taste

For the beef:
2 8-ounce Certified Angus Beef
skirt steaks

For the garnish:
Parsley
Red bell peppers

For the marinade, combine all ingredients and bring to a boil. Let simmer and reduce slowly to half the volume.

For the beef, let skirt steaks come to room temperature, then pour some of the cooled marinade on top. Let sit for approximately 1 hour. Remove from marinade and grill over high heat until you have the right doneness. Brush one more time with the marinade and serve with a salad. Garnish with parsley and red bell peppers.

JAMES MILLER

MEDALLIONS OF BEEF MEXICANA

(Serves 4)

Crescent
Metal
Products Inc.
Cleveland,
Ohio

For the dish:
1 tablespoon butter
1 cup onion, chopped
1 cup red pepper, chopped
1 cup green pepper, chopped
1/2 cup tomato concasse
1/2 cup hot beef stock
1 tablespoon tomato paste
1/2 teaspoon salt
1/8 teaspoon white pepper

1/8 teaspoon hot pepper sauce
8 4-ounce Certified Angus Beef
tenderloin medallions
1/2 teaspoon fresh ground black
pepper
2 tablespoons vegetable oil
2 tablespoons tequila
1/8 teaspoon cayenne pepper
1/4 teaspoon salt

Heat butter in sauté pan. Add onion and sauté to golden brown. Add red pepper, green pepper and tomato. Simmer 2 minutes. Blend stock and tomato paste; add to vegetables. Add salt, white pepper and hot pepper sauce. Cover and simmer for 10 minutes. While vegetables are simmering, rub beef medallions with crushed black pepper. Heat vegetable oil in a skillet. Sear meat for 3 minutes on each side. Place vegetables on pre-heated platter and put cooked medallions on top. Keep warm.

Pour off grease from the skillet and deglaze with tequila. Scrape to remove fond. Season with cayenne pepper and salt. Pour over meat and serve.

SHORT RIBS A L'ORANGE

(Serves 16)

For the short ribs:
2 tablespoons vegetable oil
8 pounds Certified Angus Beef
short ribs
Flour for dredging
5 cups fresh orange juice
3 1/2 cups beef stock
1/2 teaspoon pepper
1 teaspoon salt
1 1/2 teaspoons ground allspice

1 1/2 teaspoons ground cinnamon
1/2 teaspoon ground cloves
1 1/2 cups pitted prunes
1 1/2 cups dried apricots
3 tablespoons cornstarch
4 oranges, peeled and sectioned
Zest from one orange, blanched

For the ribs, heat oil in a large skillet. Dust ribs in flour and brown on all sides. Place meat in braising pan or large Dutch oven. Add 4 1/2 cups of the orange juice, beef stock, pepper, salt, allspice, cinnamon and cloves. Bring to a boil, cover, reduce heat and simmer for 1 1/2 hours. Skim fat. Add prunes and apricots. Mix to blend. Cover and cook for 1 hour. Skim fat. Combine cornstarch with 1/2 cup remaining orange juice, add to broth and stir. Turn onto serving plates. Garnish with orange sections and blanched zest.

JHN M^C CORMICK

JT SMOKED BEEF BRISKET WITH LOGANBERRY ESSENCE

(Serves 6)

etroit
thletic Club
etroit,
ichigan

For the loganberry essence:
1 1/2 cups loganberries or black
 raspberries
1/4 cup brandy
1 teaspoon black peppercorns
1 cup beef broth
1/4 cup honey
1 cup unsalted butter, cut into bits

For the beef:
1 3-pound Certified Angus Beef
 brisket, cut into two pieces

For the marinade:
1/2 cup Indonesian soy sauce
2 tablespoons Dijon mustard
1 1/2 cups red wine
1 tablespoon plus 1 teaspoon
 pickling spice
2 tablespoons salt

For the garnish:
Fresh basil leaves
Fresh loganberries or black
 raspberries
Stuffed cherry tomatoes

For the beef, cut off excess fat to 1/4-inch.

For the marinade, combine ingredients. Rub mixture into meat and refrigerate overnight. Turn occasionally. Make a stove top smoker using a heavy bottomed pan. Place a small pile of wood chips

(apple, hickory or cherry) in the bottom. Place a rack about 8 inches above the wood chips by using an inverted smaller pan in center. Put pan on top of range. Turn to high heat until wood chips start to smoke. Place brisket pieces on the rack and cover with top or with aluminum foil. Turn heat down to medium and smoke 15 minutes. (Do this in a well ventilated kitchen or outside on barbecue grill).

Remove brisket pieces from smoker and place on aluminum foil. Seal and make an air-tight package. Place in a preheated 350 degree F oven and cook until done to your liking.

For the loganberry essence, heat berries in a non-aluminum pan until juices start to be released. Add brandy and flambé. Add peppercorns, broth and honey. Reduce by half. Strain mixture through a fine sieve. Incorporate the butter a small amount at a time. Keep warm.

To serve, slice brisket. Pour sauce onto plates and top with beef slices. Garnish with basil, berries and stuffed tomatoes.

STEAK AND MOREL PUDDING

(Serves 6)

For the crust:
10 ounces toasted bread crumbs
5 tablespoons butter
5 tablespoons vegetable shortening
3/4 teaspoon freshly ground pepper
1/2 to 3/4 cup cold water

To assemble:
Bread crumbs
Egg yolk, beaten

For the filling:
1 cup Madeira
1/4 cup dried tarragon
1 quart heavy cream
1 cup beef broth
Salt and pepper to taste
3 tablespoons butter
36 shallots, minced
8 ounces Certified Angus Beef
 top round, cooked rare and cubed
1 cup fresh morel mushrooms,
 cleaned

For the garnish:
Steamed and seasoned snow peas
Fresh tarragon sprigs
Morel mushrooms, steamed and
 seasoned
Piped, pureed acorn squash

For the crust, rub butter and shortening into toasted bread crumbs. Add pepper. Add enough cold water for mixture to come together into a ball when squeezed with your hand. Grease 6 molds with shor-

tening. Press in crumb mixture. Place circular cutter (the size of mold opening) on a piece of wax paper and pat in filling to form the top. Chill or freeze.

For the filling, pour Madeira into non-aluminum pan and add tarragon. Reduce over moderate heat to a syrupy consistency. Add cream and broth. Reduce until mixture coats the back of a spoon. Season with salt and pepper. Set aside.

In separate pan, melt butter and lightly sauté shallots until coated. Place pan in preheated 450 degree F oven and cook 15 minutes. When lightly browned, remove pan and pour off excess butter. Pour cream mixture from above into pan with shallots. Deglaze for 1 to 2 minutes over low heat scraping bottom of pan. Remove from the heat, add beef and mushrooms. Coat well with sauce. Spoon mixture into molds and fill three-quarters full. Egg wash top of crust and place chilled tops to cover molds. Bake in a 450 degree F oven for 30 minutes.

To serve, unmold puddings onto plates. Garnish with pea pods, tarragon, morel mushrooms and puree of acorn squash.

SMOKED BEEF HASH WITH CHILI SAUCE

(Serves 4)

For the dish:
2 cups beef broth
1/2 cup clarified butter
12 large potato balls, blanched
16 large cubes carrots, blanched
1 pound smoked Certified Angus
 Beef brisket, cut into large cubes
16 pearl onions, blanched
8 olive-shaped zucchini balls
8 olive-shaped yellow squash balls
3 cups prepared chili sauce

Heat half of the beef broth in a sauté pan and add clarified butter. Bring to a boil. Add potatoes and cook a few minutes. Add carrots and reduce liquid until almost dry. Add beef cubes. Stir and scrape bottom of pan. When beef and vegetables begin to turn brown, add remainder of broth. Scrape bottom well. When reduced again, add pearl onions. Stir and add squash. Toss or stir in pan until golden brown.

In a separate pan bring chili sauce to a boil. Ladle out onto plates and top with hash. Garnish with parsley.

WILLIAM HAHNE

SHORT RIB STEW, MAIN STREET

(Serves 4)

*Boggstown Inn
and Cabaret*

Boggstown Inn
and Caberet
Boggstown,
Indiana

For the stew:
6 tablespoons all-purpose flour
1 tablespoon herb seasoning
1 teaspoon cayenne pepper
4 pounds Certified Angus Beef
    short ribs, cut into 3-inch portions
1/4 cup vegetable oil
2 cups beer
1 cup coffee
2 bay leaves
1 teaspoon thyme
1 teaspoon rosemary
1 tablespoon beef base
8 very small onions, peeled
Carrots, steamed
Red and white potatoes, steamed
Turnips, steamed

For the garnish:
Sprigs of fresh rosemary

For the stew, combine flour, herb seasoning and cayenne pepper. Evenly coat short ribs in the flour mixture. In a large heavy pot, heat oil and brown the short ribs. Slowly add beer, coffee, bay leaves, thyme, rosemary and beef base to the ribs. Bring to a boil, then cover and simmer for 1 1/2 hours. Add onions to stew and cook for 30 minutes.

To serve, place the stew in large soup plates. Top with steamed portions of carrots, red and white potatoes and turnips. Garnish with sprigs of fresh rosemary.

GERHARD BRILL

GRILLADES AND GRITS

(Serves 4)

Perdido Beach
Hilton Resort
Orange Beach,
Alabama

For the beef:
1 3/4 pounds Certified Angus Beef
    bottom sirloin butt, ball tip
2 teaspoons salt
1 teaspoon freshly ground black
    pepper
1/8 teaspoon cayenne pepper
1 tablespoon finely minced garlic
2 tablespoons all-purpose flour
1 1/2 tablespoons lard
1 cup chopped onion
1 large ripe Creole, beefsteak or
    Jersey tomato, coarsely chopped
1 cup water, more if necessary,
    or beef stock
3 cups cooked grits

For the beef, trim all the fat off the meat. Cut into pieces about 2 inches square and pound out with a mallet to about 4 inches square. Rub the salt, black pepper, cayenne and garlic into the pieces of meat on both sides, then rub in the flour. In a large heavy skillet or sauté pan, melt the lard over the heat and brown the grillades well on both sides. Lower the heat and add the onion, tomato, water or beef stock. Bring to a simmer, cover loosely, and cook over low heat for about 30 minutes, uncovering to turn the meat over every 10 minutes. A rich brown gravy will form during cooking; if it appears too thick, add water a little bit at a time. When the meat is cooked, remove it to a heated plat-

ter and place in a preheated 200 degree oven to keep warm. Prepare the grits according to package directions. Just before serving reheat the gravy in the skillet, then pour it over both the meat and the grits.

C.T. NICE

SERVICE AMERICA
CORPORATION

Certified Angus Beef is indeed Presidential fare. At the January 1989 inauguration of President George Bush in Washington, D.C., members of the Houston (Texas) Chef's Association prepared Certified Angus Beef briskets for the inauguration dinner. The Houston Certified Angus Beef food service distributor provides President Bush with beef for his barbecues held around the world. One such barbecue was in Houston last spring where C.T. Nice, chef of the George Brown Convention Center, created Certified Angus Beef Flank Steak with Chorizo Sausage for the President and his 800 guests. The recipe follows.

FLANK STEAK WITH CHORIZO SAUSAGE

(Serves 4)

George R.
Brown
Convention
Center
Houston,
Texas

For the chorizo sausage:
1/2 teaspoon ground cumin
1 teaspoon paprika
1/4 teaspoon cayenne pepper
Salt to taste
1/4 teaspoon black pepper
2 tablespoons chopped parsley
1 tablespoon chopped cilantro
1/4 cup red wine
2 eggs, beaten
5 ounces coarsely ground beef
5 ounces coarsely ground pork

For the beef:
1 1/2 to 2 pounds Certified Angus
    Beef flank steak
2 tablespoons oil

For the garnish:
2 red bell peppers, cored, seeded
    and cut into brunoise
1/4 pound plum tomatoes, peeled,
    seeded and cut into brunoise

For the sausage, dissolve all spices and herbs in red wine. Add beaten eggs. Mix this thoroughly with ground beef and pork. Set aside.

For the beef, pound flank steak to 3/4-inch thickness. Spread chorizo sausage over entire surface of flank steak. Roll and tie, being careful to maintain the pinwheel effect. Sear in hot oil, then roast in a 350 degree F oven to an internal temperature of 145 degrees, about 20 to 25 minutes. Let rest 1 hour.

Slice and garnish with red pepper and tomato brunoise.

OE MANNKE

XAS STEAK TIPS WITH SCRAMBLED EGGS

(erves 6)

otisserie for
eef and Bird
ouston,
exas

For the beef:
1 1/2 pounds Certified Angus Beef
sirloin tips (cut into strips)
Salt and pepper to taste
4 tablespoons butter or margarine
4 cloves garlic, peeled and minced

For the eggs:
1/2 cup corn oil
6 slices bread (Italian or sourdough)
8 eggs, beaten
1/2 cup milk or half and half
1 tablespoon Worcestershire sauce
6 drops hot pepper sauce

For the garnish:
Chopped cilantro

For the sirloin tips, season the meat with salt and pepper, place the butter in a heavy skillet and heat over medium-heat until sizzling. Brown meat on both sides and combine with the garlic. Remove from the pan and keep warm, and reserve the pan drippings. Heat the oil in another pan, add the bread and fry quickly on both sides. Drain on a paper towel and keep warm. Scramble the eggs in the oil left in the second skillet, and at the same time add milk or half and half into the first pan, season with Worcestershire and hot pepper sauce. Bring to a boil. Stir to loosen browned bits from the bottom of the pan and simmer to reduce the liquid.

For serving, arrange the bread on heated individual serving plates, then top with beef, scrambled eggs and hot pepper sauce. Garnish with chopped cilantro.

EXAS STEAK SALAD

(erves 6)

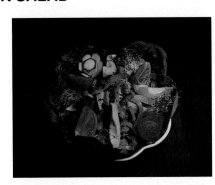

For the salad:
1 1/2 pounds lean roasted Certified
Angus Beef top round (inside)
4 tablespoons chives, chopped
1 cup Italian salad dressing
1 1/2 heads romaine lettuce

For the garnish:
3 ripe avocados, peeled and wedged
Alfalfa sprouts
Tomato wedges
Radishes

For the salad, slice the top round of beef and then cut into julienne strips. Combine the beef, chopped chives and Italian dressing. Refrigerate for two hours. Wash the lettuce and place in 6 individual bowls. Portion the marinated beef over the lettuce. Garnish with avocado, tomato wedges, alfalfa sprouts and radishes. Serve with toasted bread.

MICHAEL GARBIN

BLACKENED FILET MIGNON SALAD

(Serves 4)

THE WIGWAM
Golf and Country Club

For the beef:
4 4-ounce Certified Angus Beef filets
1/2 cup blackened seasoning mixture

For the garnish:
Vinaigrette dressing
Garlic toast

For the salad:
1 head baby red oak lettuce
1 head baby red romaine lettuce
1 head baby romaine lettuce
1 Belgian endive
4 bunches mâche
1 head radicchio
1/4 head frisée
4 plum tomatoes, sliced
24 orange segments

For the salad, chill four dinner plates. Wash and separate leaves of lettuces and wrap in paper towels to dry. Arrange assorted greens on plates. Arrange tomato slices and orange segments on plates. Chill until ready to serve.

For the beef, slightly flatten filets and coat with blackened seasoning on both sides. Sear in a fry pan or cook on a charcoal grill until desired doneness. Let filets rest 5 minutes for juices to settle. Slice beef and arrange on plates. Serve with dressing and garlic toast.

PAILLARD OF BEEF WITH WILD MUSHROOMS

(Serves 4)

The Wigwam
Resort
Litchfield Park,
Arizona

For the beef:
4 8-ounce Certified Angus Beef strip
loin steaks
1 tablespoon chopped garlic
3/4 cup olive oil
1/2 teaspoon minced fresh thyme
1 teaspoon minced cilantro
2 tablespoons cracked black
peppercorns
Salt and freshly ground pepper

For the garnish:
Roasted new potatoes
Fresh, steamed and seasoned
vegetables

For the remainder of dish:
1/4 cup olive oil
4 tablespoons sliced shallots
1 cup sliced shiitake mushrooms
1 cup sliced chanterelle mushrooms
1 cup sliced oyster mushrooms
1 teaspoon minced fresh thyme
1 tablespoon chopped cilantro
Salt and freshly ground black pepper

For the beef, flatten steaks that have been totally cleaned of fat and silver skin with a meat mallet. Place steaks in a shallow pan. Combine garlic, olive oil, thyme, cilantro and cracked black pepper and pour over steaks. This can be done 2 to 6 hours in advance of cooking.

Remove steaks from marinade. Season with salt and pepper and cook over charcoal or in a fry pan until desired doneness.

Meanwhile, heat olive oil in sauté pan. Add shallots and sauté until transparent. Add mushrooms and quickly toss in pan. Add thyme, cilantro and season with salt and pepper. To serve, spoon mushroom sauce onto plate. Slice steaks and shingle slices over sauce. Serve with potatoes and fresh vegetables.

PATRIZIO SACCHETTO

ROULADE OF BEEF WITH ASPARAGUS

(Serves 6)

The Blue Fox
San Francisco,
California

For the beef:
2 pounds Certified Angus Beef flank steak
Salt and pepper to taste
Caul fat
30 asparagus spears, blanched

For the red bell pepper mousse:
1 1/2 pounds pork or beef trimmings, ground and chilled
1 clove garlic
Rosemary
Thyme
Salt and pepper to taste
1 tablespoon brandy
3/4 cup puree of roasted red pepper
1 1/2 egg whites

For the sauce:
Mirepoix of onions, celery and carrots
Rosemary
Thyme
1/2 cup red wine
2 cups veal demi-glace

For the yellow bell pepper mousse:
1/2 pound Certified Angus Beef trimmings, ground and chilled
1/2 cup puree of roasted yellow pepper
1 1/2 egg whites
1/2 cup heavy cream
Salt and pepper to taste

For the beef, butterfly, then slightly pound the flank and cut into 4 inch by 7 inch, 5-ounce pieces and season with salt and pepper. Lay out a strip of caul fat, roughly 5 inches by 7 inches. Spread a layer of red bell pepper mousse on the caul fat, approximately 1/4-inch thick. Then place the prepared flank on top of the mousse and spread a thin layer of the yellow bell pepper mousse on the flank. Place five spears of the blanched asparagus on the mousse and pipe a small amount of yellow bell pepper mousse down the center of the five

spears, lengthwise. Roll into a roulade that both ends of the flank and red mousse are touching, and the caul fat slightly overlapping. Truss with butcher string, season with salt and pepper, se in frying pan and roast at 350 degrees until mousse in center is set, approximately 15 minutes.

For the red pepper mousse, place ground beef or pork, garlic, herbs, salt, pepper and brandy in food processor, a work until all the ingredients become pasty. Add the pureed peppers and process until the mixture becomes smooth. Add the egg whites and puree a smooth, but stiff, mousse.

For the yellow bell pepper mousse, prepare the same way as for the red be pepper mousse except add the cream a the end of the procedure.

For the sauce, sweat the mirepoix. A the herbs and red wine. Reduce by half and add the demi-glace and bring to a s mer. Slightly puree and strain. Season with salt and pepper.

BOLLITO MISTO (MIXED BOIL)

(Serves 6 to 8)

For the dish:
2 to 3 pounds assorted Certified Angus Beef parts (flank, sirloin butt or chuck)
1 clove
1 fresh bay leaf
6 black peppercorns
2 onions
4 to 5 large leeks
2 carrots, peeled
1 tablespoon unflavored gelatin
Salt and pepper to taste

For the garnish:
Italian mustard fruit

For the beef, in a large stock pot, cover meat with water. Add clove, bay leaf, black peppercorns, onion, leeks and carrots, and simmer. Remove leeks and carrots when they are tender. Continue to cook meat until tender and then remove meat from stock. Let cool and remove any sinew or fat from meat. Cut the meat into cubes or strips adequate in size for form-

ing the terrine. Strain the stock the meat was boiled in and reduce to one quart. Whisk in gelatin. Season with salt and pepper. Let cool, but not set.

Line an 8 inch by 4 inch terrine with plastic wrap and a layer of leeks, and sta pressing in the mixture of meats alternat ing with carrots, leeks and the gelatin mi ture. When the terrine is full place a laye of leek on top and refrigerate until set.

To serve, slice and garnish with mustard fruit.

BECHAMEL SAUCE

(Yields 1 cup)

**For Cured Flank
Steak with Spicy
Shrimp Recipe
from page 70**

2 tablespoons butter
2 tablespoons flour
1 cup milk, warmed
1 small onion, studded with 3 cloves
1/2 bay leaf
Salt to taste
Pinch of nutmeg

Melt the butter in a saucepan over low heat. Add the flour and blend well for 5 minutes. Remove from heat and cool. Slowly stir in the warmed milk, and add the onion and bay leaf. Cook and stir with a wooden spoon until sauce thickens and coats the back of the spoon. Place in a preheated oven at 350 degrees F for 20

minutes. Remove from the oven and stra the sauce. Season with salt and nutmeg to taste.

THOMAS SEMKE

HAZELNUT ROSEMARY PINWHEEL

(Serves 4)

Multnomah
Athletic Club
Portland,
Oregon

For the filling:
1 1/2 cups hazelnuts, ground fine
1 bunch fresh rosemary, chopped fine
2 cloves garlic, minced fine
Salt and pepper to taste
Fresh bread crumbs to bind

For the beef:
2 pounds Certified Angus Beef bottom sirloin butt, tri-tip , butterflied and pounded to 1/4-inch thickness
All-purpose flour
1 tablespoon oil

For the dish, mix the hazelnuts with the fresh rosemary, garlic, and salt and pepper. Add the fresh bread crumbs enough

to help bind the product. Spread the mixture over the thin pounded meat, leaving at least one-inch border of meat. Roll as tightly as possible and secure with a toothpick. Dust in all-purpose flour and brown in a small amount of oil. Place in a roasting pan and bake at 350 degrees F approximately 20 to 25 minutes or until you reach an internal temperature of 130 degrees. Slice and serve.

THOMAS SEMKE

BEEF ITALIANO

(Serves 4)

For the sauce:
4 tablespoons minced onions
2 tablespoons butter
2 tablespoons dry white wine
1 cup brown sauce
1 tablespoon chopped sour pickles
1 tablespoon chopped capers
Salt and pepper to taste
1 teaspoon Dijon mustard
Pinch of powdered sugar

For the beef:
4 8-ounce Certified Angus Beef
  strip loin steaks
Salt and pepper
2 tablespoons oil
1/2 cup coarse-grain mustard
4 slices fresh bread, crumbed into
  fresh bread crumbs
1 clove garlic, minced
1/4 cup chopped parsley
Olive oil

For the sauce, place butter in a sauce pan and saute onions until lightly browned. Add the white wine and cook until the liquid is almost evaporated. Add the brown sauce and simmer 10 minutes. Strain and season with salt and pepper. Just before serving, add the pickles, capers, mustard and powdered sugar.

For the beef, season steaks with salt and pepper. Place in a hot skillet with oil and sear until browned. Brush the steaks with the mustard and roll the steaks in the mixture of fresh bread crumbs, garlic and chopped parsley. Drizzle the steaks with a small amount of olive oil and bake to medium-rare, about 4-6 minutes, in a 375 degree F oven. Serve in the mustard sauce.

WILLIAM JUNG

FOUR ONION COLORADO CHILI

(Serves 6)

Harry's
Soup & Chowder Company
Clackamas,
Oregon

For the beef:
3/4 cup olive oil
5 pounds Certified Angus Beef
  bottom round (outside) or chuck,
  cut in 1-inch cubes
1/2 pound salt pork, trimmed, diced
  and lightly blanched

For the spices:
1 tablespoon black peppercorns
1 tablespoon white peppercorns
2 teaspoons red chili flakes
4 large bay leaves
3 tablespoons dried oregano or
  1/4 cup fresh
3/4 cup ground Colorado chili powder
1/4 cup paprika
4 tablespoons cumin powder

For the vegetables:
2 cups chopped green bell peppers
2 cups chopped celery with leaves
4 cups chopped onions
2 cups chopped leeks
1/2 cup chopped garlic
4 tablespoons minced shallots
1/2 cup chopped jalapeño pepper

To finish:
2 cups diced, fresh plum tomatoes
5 cups beer
1/4 cup vinegar
1/4 cup lime juice
1/2 cup masa harina (if you don't
  have it, use corn tortillas or chips
  soaked with hot water for 10
  minutes and pureed in blender)

For the beef, heat oil in a large, heavy sauce or roasting pan. Add beef and salt pork and brown well. Then add the vegetables. Continue to saute for approximately 5 minutes.

For the spices, grind black and white peppercorns, chili flakes, bay leaves, and oregano in a coffee mill. Add ground mixture to meat and vegetables. Add Colorado chili powder, paprika and cumin. Continue to sauté 10 minutes. Then add plum tomatoes, beer, vinegar, lime juice and masa harina and bring to boil, stirring constantly. Lower heat and simmer until meat is tender and sauce is smooth - approximately 2 to 3 hours. If too thick, add more beer or good strong beef stock as needed.

HOISIN BEEF

(Serves 4)

For the beef and marinade:
1 14-ounce Certified Angus Beef top
  sirloin butt cap muscle
1 quart vegetable oil
2 tablespoons salt
1 teaspoon coriander
1 teaspoon cumin
1 tablespoon freshly ground black
  pepper

For the hoisin marinade:
2 cups hoisin sauce
2 tablespoons minced garlic
2 cups chicken stock
1 cup sugar
1/2 cup soy sauce
1 1/2 tablespoons Chinese five-spice
  powder
2 tablespoons red food coloring
1/2 cup dry sherry
2 cups dry sherry

For the chinese mustard:
1 cup Coleman's dry mustard
1/4 teaspoon sesame oil
1 teaspoon soy sauce
Enough rice wine vinegar to make
  smooth paste

For the hot and sour sauce:
1/2 cup seasoned rice vinegar
1/2 cup fresh lime juice
1 tablespoon sambal oelek
1 teaspoon fresh minced ginger

For the garnish:
Toasted sesame seeds
Hoisin sauce
Pickled baby ginger

For the beef and marinade, combine marinade ingredients and marinate for 3 or more days.

Remove beef from marinade and wipe off excess oil. Combine hoisin sauce, garlic, chicken stock, sugar and soy sauce. Heat until well blended. Remove from heat and add five spice powder, red food coloring and 1/2 cup dry sherry. Pour over meat and chill at least 3 days and up to 7 days.

Remove meat from marinade (wipe off excess and reserve marinade for basting) and cook using either of the following methods: a) broil over mesquite or kava wood grill for approximately 5 minutes for each side, or b) place on a wire rack in roasting pan (at least 2 inches from bottom of pan) and place in a preheated, slow oven (275 degrees F). Add 2 cups of dry sherry to bottom of pan. Bake approximately 45 - 60 minutes, basting occasionally with hoisin marinade. Make sure liquid in bottom of pan does not evaporate.

For the Chinese mustard, combine mustard powder, sesame oil, soy sauce and enough vinegar to make a smooth paste.

For the hot and sour sauce, combine rice vinegar, lime juice, sambal oelek and ginger.

To serve, thinly slice on the diagonal and serve with the Chinese mustard, toasted sesame seeds, hoisin sauce, hot and sour sauce and pickled baby ginger.

Recipe Index